A Teacher's Project Guide
to the
Internet

A Teacher's Project Guide
to the
Internet

Kevin R. Crotchett

HEINEMANN ◆ Portsmouth, NH

Heinemann
A division of Reed Elsevier Inc.
361 Hanover Street
Portsmouth, NH 03801-3912

Offices and agents throughout the world

The author and publisher wish to thank those who have generously given permission to reprint borrowed material:

Figure 1–1 by Donna Cox and Robert Patterson, courtesy of NCSA, University of Illinois at Urbana-Champaign.

Library of Congress Cataloging-in-Publication Data

Crotchett, Kevin R.
    A teacher's project guide to the Internet / Kevin R. Crotchett.
        p.   cm.
    Includes bibliographical references (p.).
    ISBN 0-435-07104-1
    1. Internet (Computer network) in education.   2. World Wide Web (Information retrieval system)   3. Electronic mail systems.
    I. Title.
    LB1044.87.C76   1997
    025.06′37—dc21   97-4068
                                                                      CIP

Editors: Leigh Peake and William Varner
Production: Renée M. Nicholls
Cover Design: Jenny Jensen Greenleaf
Manufacturing: Louise Richardson

Printed in the United States of America on acid-free paper

00 99 98 97   EB   1 2 3 4 5 6

To my wife, Tracy, for her love, support, and presence;
To my mother, for her lifelong guidance;
To Joe, for his spirit and inspiration; and
To all the children from Room 13
who have allowed me to walk and learn
alongside them.

Contents

Contents

Contents

Acknowledgments

This book never would have existed without the encouragement and support of some very dear friends and cherished colleagues. I am extremely grateful to Deborah Walters, who provided me with the inspiration and encouragement that only a true professional mentor and friend can. I would like to thank Sandra Wilde for generously mentoring me through the writing process with words of wisdom and friendship. To Jackie Bidney, who tediously reviewed every page, many thanks. Thanks also to Tawnya Luethe, David Lifton, and Joe Maddocks for their input and guidance on various chapters.

I am deeply indebted to Leigh Peake, Bill Varner, Renée Nicholls, and the rest of the Heinemann team, who aided me throughout the writing process, guiding me into unfamiliar territory and easing my nerves. Finally, this book would not have been possible without the loving support of my wife, Tracy Crotchett, and the children of Room 13, who provided me with the imagination and inspiration that made this book a reality.

ONE

The Internet and the Classroom: Preparing for Your Voyage

Imagine a morning beginning with a trip to the Louvre. As you escort your class through the halls of fine art, you end up in front of Leonardo da Vinci's *Mona Lisa*. After studying the painting for some time and discussing it with your students, you leave the Louvre for a meeting with art experts and enthusiasts from around the world. During this meeting, you and your students gain a perspective on the da Vinci piece that none of you had discovered while at the museum. Soon, your guests depart, and you are left with a room filled with creative young minds. Turning to your canvas of choice, butcher paper, your students begin to cover and fill the blank sheets with their own imagery, similar to that of the *Mona Lisa*, rich with color and depth, thick with paint and movement. After the students complete their own works of art, they turn to the world to share their thoughts about their experiences this morning.

This scenario is far from fiction. With the tools provided by current technology, it is not difficult for students to visit places such as the Louvre, to speak to artists and art enthusiasts regarding a piece of fine art, or to converse with the world about their impressions of the *Mona Lisa*. The following day could open with new possibilities for this classroom. Now that their artwork is dry, it could easily be displayed beside the *Mona Lisa*, complete with a comparison of the two pieces written by the classroom artists. Responses to the students' work could begin to flow into the classroom literally from around the world. These responses could spark discussion and artistic controversy, forming new connections for you and your students. All of this and much more is reality and it is all a benefit of membership in the Internet's global community.

The Internet is truly beginning to affect every aspect of our lives—business, government, home, and school. In the past twelve months, the Internet has become a weekly mention on the evening news, both local and national. News reports focusing on the many legal and social implications of Internet use have become commonplace. During this time, we have also seen an increase in legislation in response to this fairly new global technology.

Only a few years ago, the business community was looking for educated individuals with highly developed personal skills and some computer knowledge. Now, in 1996, businesses are actively seeking individuals not only with advanced personal and computer skills, but also with the knowledge of network systems including email, file sharing, Internet protocol, and the basic operation of Internet tools. With this increase in the need for technologically skilled individuals comes the need to increase the amount of education and experience students have with regard to computer technology and electronic networking, specifically the Internet. Schools at all levels are quickly upgrading their computer equipment and gaining access to the Internet. With such access, students are able to work on the Information Super Highway, performing a variety of tasks and searching the Internet for both educational and entertainment purposes.

While this expansion in global technology has been led by the business, government, and commercial leaders of the world, it has in many respects left educators outside the electronic link. There are, however, a large number of educational tools and resources available to educators via the Internet, many of which are suited to the needs of the teacher, while others are designed for students. The question for educators is not "Should we get our students on the Internet?" but rather "What should we have our students do on the Internet?" The following chapters will aid in answering the latter question. Beginning with an introduction to a basic Internet tool, email, and expanding to more advanced skill-based technologies, such as writing

Hypertext Markup Language (HTML) documents for the World Wide Web (WWW), this book provides you with Internet-based activities that can be implemented with students at all educational levels with varying degrees of planning. As you work through the chapters, each taking you further into the Internet, you can begin to use more of the Internet itself by combining newsgroups with email or WWW surfing with student-published WWW works and HTML homepages. Most important, the chapters will start you on a journey through the Internet via student projects, allowing your students to gain essential Internet experience by means of curriculum integration.

How to Use This Book

The chapters herein take you from one of the most basic Internet functions, email, to one of the more difficult, writing WWW homepages, with intervening chapters that describe projects using Usenet Newsgroups, File Transfer Protocols (FTP), Gopher, Veronica, the World Wide Web, and Internet Search Engines. The order that the chapters are in allows you and your students the opportunity to build on previous knowledge and experiences. Some of you may wish to start with the first chapter and become more comfortable with those activities before moving on to the next Internet function, while others may find that the best use of this text is simply to pull out your favorite projects and activities. The choice will depend upon your experience with the Internet and your comfort level with the different tools and functions of the Internet.

"So, What Should I Aready Know and What Do I Need to Get Started?"

At the introduction of each chapter, basic information is given about the Internet tool that will be the primary focus for that chapter. This information is not meant to be a step-by-step, how-to menu; rather it is simply an overview and history of that function of the Internet. The number of available Internet servers, computer platforms (Macintosh, DOS, Windows, and UNIX), software programs, and network managers are far too numerous for this book to cover in-depth. While you do not need to be an Internaut (a highly experienced Internet user) to use this project guide, some basic experience with the Internet will be helpful. While bookstore shelves have little to offer educators about the Internet, they have literally hundreds of more general Internet guides and how-to books to help every Internet user get started.

At a minimum, you will need an email account to implement the student projects described within. The more extensive your Internet access, the more project ideas you will be able to use. Your Internet connection may not even need to be in your classroom or building. Many email, newsgroup, and WWW projects can easily be implemented via the "Sneaker-Net" method. By using your home computer connected to the Internet, you can download articles, email, and newsgroup posts, saving them to disk. That disk can then be used in compatible computers in your classroom. Students can save their corresponding email and newsgroup post on the same disk, which can be uploaded to the Internet once you have returned to the Internet-connected computer. The term "Sneaker-Net" was coined to indicate the method by which the information is traveling: shoes. Though this method requires "home work" for you, it is often the easiest solution to connection problems in the classroom.

The Connected Classroom: Social Concerns

Classrooms connected to or seeking a connection on the Internet quickly become aware of the social/ethical controversy that surrounds this amazing technology. The Internet itself is still very much in its infancy. The road ahead on the Informational Super Highway has yet to be built and though the blueprints are still being questioned, the construction of this highway has commenced. As with any new technology that promises to alter society as we know it, the Internet has entered the world of media sensationalism, political debate, and social controversy. When the horseless carriage was introduced in the late 1800s, the general population feared the new automobile. When television was introduced to the United States in the 1930s, society responded with fear of social breakdown until the technology was widely accepted ten years later. When humans traveled beyond the gravitational pull of the Earth, many people responded with fears of future space travel. Now, the population is responding to another new technology, the Internet, often with the same hesitation and fear of the unknown.

The news media would like us to believe that the Internet is filled with predators and pornographers just waiting to download their questionable material and information into our homes, businesses, and classrooms. Politicians would also like us to follow the notion that the Internet is a technology that is out of control, a form of mass media and information that needs to be censored and moderated. In fact, the negative aspects of the Internet are minor when compared to the wealth of productive, entertaining, and educational information it offers. While the media is quick to announce the latest news on email harassment and chat-line predators, and politicians are ready to write new legislation and enact national censorship laws across an international network, they fail to mention the thousands of NASA Internet sites or the hundreds of on-line libraries, colleges, and universities throughout the world.

Regardless of current or future censorship legislation, it is essential that children working on the Internet are taught limits and restraints with regard to information retrieval. Internet providers and new software products that limit the type of access Internet users receive are quickly becoming available. These services and software products make it possible for schools and households to restrict access to known Internet sites that have undesirable material. While these forms of censoring the Internet may make administrators and parents feel more secure, they will never replace the personal sense of responsibility and etiquette that one should learn when using this technology. It is for that reason that I strongly believe that with any classroom or household Internet connection, a curriculum and agreement in netiquette (Internet etiquette) must be taught and practiced.

With the start of the new school year, my fourth- and fifth-grade students are introduced to the classroom in the form of a tour. This introduction makes for the foundation of the classroom rules and agreements. It is during this tour that the students are introduced to the classroom's computer station. As a group, they brainstorm proper behaviors that should be observed when working around or in this area. As this list of behaviors is refined, the students' language is adopted by the classroom and made into a computer contract, also known as an Acceptable Use Policy (AUP). The first portion of our AUP contains rules for computer use, such as appropriate times, uses, and treatment of the equipment. The second portion defines the information and data that can be found on the computers or retrieved over the Internet.

Students are taught to work with only their computer files and those files that are intended for whole classroom use. This process generally takes place in the form of small-group and whole class discussions. As the class begins to utilize the Internet, the discussions turn to information retrieval. These lessons include topics such as informational screening and age-appropriate Internet access. Through these lessons, students are encouraged to surf the Internet by using a list of pre-approved Internet sites. These sites often contain links to other sites that allow students to independently investigate and explore the Internet. As students surf to new sites off the class list, they put to use a student-written and -adopted protocol to judge the sites' usefulness and appropriateness in the classroom (see Chapter 6, The World Wide Web). It is this guided freedom that aids in teaching students about the importance of their responsibility and the need to maintain an age-appropriate outlook on the Internet.

Critics of AUP and netiquette curriculums that allow for free online student exploration take the position that such curriculums only point out to students the existence of inappropriate material on the Internet, making it more inviting. The reality is that students are already familiar with the darker side of the Internet. The media at large has exposed this side of the Internet in detail, often highlighting it on prime time news and entertainment programming. An AUP and netiquette curriculum that confronts this darker Internet up front provides students with guidance and limitations, aids in building independent lifelong responsibility, and allows guided yet independent exploration and creativity to foster.

Many school districts adopt a type of AUP and netiquette curriculum with their Internet connectivity. It is my contention that this curriculum should go one step further and be built into student assessment. In our classroom, students' assessment of their computer and technology use is accompanied by fulfillment of their AUP contract and by the practice of appropriate computer use and demonstration of learned netiquette skills.

AUP contracts are signed by the student, the parents, and the teacher. They should clearly state expected behaviors and expected uses of the computer station, and they should define the circumstances that may result in consequences, including the removal of one's right to computer and/or Internet access. Throughout the year, the terms of this contract are reviewed. While many districts are putting such AUPs to use, some are gaining connectivity prior to writing an AUP or a netiquette curriculum. If your district or your individual school has not yet acquired such a curriculum, I recommend that individual classrooms take steps to create their own in order to better define the roles and objectives of technology use to parents and the community. You can find examples of AUP contracts on the Internet by turning your Web browser or Gopher menu to the ERIC data base at "gopher://ericir.syr.edu:70/11/Guides/Agreements" or search Rice University in Houston, Texas, at "gopher://riceinfo.rice.edu:1170/11/More/Acceptable" (see Chapter 5 and Chapter 6 for more information about accessing Gopher and WWW).

History of the Internet

Surprisingly enough, the Internet has been around in one form or another for nearly thirty years. It all started in the late 1960s when a number of computer scientists wished to link computers together so that data and information could flow back and forth at great speeds. Originally, this required that each computer have a direct cable link to every other computer on the network. Considering the Internet of today, this would mean that each computer connected to the Internet would have millions of cables coming from the back, each connecting it to one other computer. This cable nightmare was solved in 1969 when research funded by the Advanced Research Projects Administration developed the Internet protocol now known as TCP/IP.

TCP/IP allows each computer to be given an address, known as the Internet Protocol (IP) address. This address can then be used to send information from one computer to another. Each address is a series of numbers, such as "123.456.78.900", separated by periods. Today, these numbers have been assigned words and letters, which are known as the domain name. This was done to accommodate the human operators of computers who prefer names and words much more than computers do. For example, a popular software archive site's address is "oak.oakland.edu". While the numerical IP address for "oak.oakland.edu" gives us little information, the domain address tell us some specific information about the computer site. Reading from right to left we discover that the computer belongs to an educational or research institution ("edu") which is connected to a network known as "oakland" and the computer itself goes by the name of "oak". If the first portion of the address was "com," we could infer that the computer belongs to a commercial organization; "gov"—a government agency; "mil"—a military operation; "net"—a major network site; "int"—an international organization; or "org"—other miscellaneous organizations. This first portion of the address can also be a two-letter abbreviation, indicating the country the computer is in. If the domain name begins with one of the three-letter combinations listed above, you can assume that the computer is in the United States. When information is sent electronically to "oak.oakland. edu", the address is reconfigured into the numeric IP system by use of a domain program found within your Internet server. In this case "oak.oakland.edu" becomes "141.210.10.117".

As we moved into the 1980s, many research facilities and educational institutions were beginning to link up to the Internet. It was at this time that the National Science Foundation (NSF) began to play a major role in spurring the Internet's growth. By using supercomputers as network servers, the NSF set up gateways for other computers to link to, later known as the NSFnet. These gateways served in

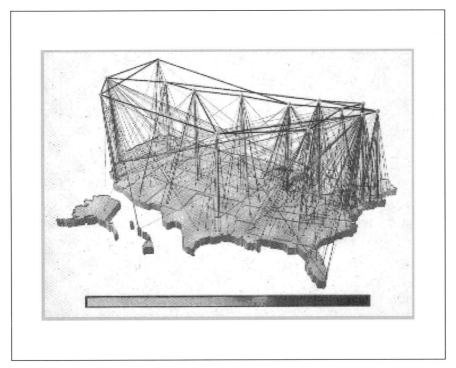

FIG. 1–1:   *NSFnet*

many respects as a central hub, a place where many smaller computer networks could link. Each gateway is linked to other gateways. As this process continued to grow, fueled by government, research, and commercial funding, networks linking to gateways linking to other gateways developed into the global network of networks, the Internet.

The largest network gateways of the Internet form the backbone of the network. As this global community grows, the number of connected computers grows with it. Figure 1–1 displays a diagram of the backbone of the NSFnet. The top level represents gateways which connect regional networks, which in turn connect smaller networks and finally individual computers. As these gateways become filled with data, the process of electronic information transfer slows down. As a result, new gateways are constantly being created and the Internet continues to grow at astonishing rates. In 1990, according to Matrix Information and Directory services, there were an estimated 56,000 Internet hosts or servers worldwide. Compare that to today's estimate of 4,652,000 Internet hosts worldwide.

The Internet has come a long way from its original three-computer network for researchers. It now spans the globe, offering its users the tools and resources needed to travel along the Information Super Highway. The Internet is truly creating a global electronic community that has no boundaries and is limited only by the future itself—a future which will continue to mold the Internet into the world's most extensive information resource. So gather up some twenty to thirty chairs, introduce a few minds to the future, log in, and enjoy the voyage.

TWO

Email: The 20,000 Mile-an-Hour Postal Service

Return-Path: fran@somewhere.else.fr
Date: Sat, 08 July 1995 10:11:36–0800
To: judy@somewhere.com
From: fran@somewhere.else.fr
Subject: Hello and a photo to come! :)

Dear Judy,

I got your message last night at 11:00 p.m., my time. From the top of your message, I was reading it only twenty-three minutes after you sent it, 10:44 a.m. your time, 6:44 p.m. my time, cool huh! My dad said he would send you a picture of me in JPG format (what ever that is), it should be attached to this email. Let me know when you get it. Next week we celebrate July 14, the Baccalaureate, France's Independence day. In my little city of Pornic we have a street dance and a small parade. How was your 4th of July? Talk to ya in a couple days. :)

Au-revoir,
Francoise

```
                                          ,,,
                                         (o o)
———————————————————————————— oOO—( )—Ooo—

Francoise Gretre                          \o_ \ / _o/
                                          _/  |   \_
fran@somewhere.else.fr                     |  /o\   |
```

The above letter will take less than fifteen minutes to reach its destination, the western United States. It will travel over 5000 miles, bouncing off one or more space satellites, crossing the entire Atlantic Ocean. In minutes the electronic impulse will reach one of the many major Internet gateways on the east coast of the United States. From there the message will be routed from gateway to gateway, network to network, at speeds greater than 20,000 miles per hour. Approximately fifteen minutes after its departure, Francoise's message will be in her keypal's electronic mailbox, waiting for Judy to log on and retrieve her friend's letter and picture from Pornic, France.

The most widely used Internet protocol happens to be one of the oldest, email. As stated in the Introduction, networking systems truly began their development back in the late 1960s. Electronic mail was born, and as the Internet has grown, the use and efficiency of email has grown as well. Today, email is the most basic Internet protocol, the most frequently used, and often the sole reason for connectivity to the Internet. Email offers Internet subscribers the ability to communicate with the world at speeds greater than any postal service can ever hope to achieve.

The Email Message : More than Meets the Eye

While the main content of an email message is contained in the body of the message, some information is also provided to the reader via the email header and the sender's email signature. Like a canceled stamp on the outside of an envelope, email headers and signatures provide you with some basic information about the sender, the date, and the time the message was sent. Looking at the email message above, you will notice that the message begins with what is called the email header. This header is fairly straightforward, giving you such information as the address from where the message was sent, known as the return path, the date and the time the message was sent, to whom it was sent, the address of the author of the message, which is normally the same as the return path, and a single-sentence subject line.

At the foot of the message, many people use signatures as a way of personalizing their electronic mail. It is often said that the Internet dehumanizes our conversations, making such communication cold and mechanical. This is far from the truth. In our human attempt to keep our conversations personal and individualized, signatures have become very popular, adding to our computer-generated messages the personal flair and individuality that typed text removes. In the example above the signature is composed of the sender's name, the sender's email address, and a couple personally chosen text pictures, called ASCII art. ASCII art has become a popular way of adding that human touch and is well liked by children. Many ASCII art sources have sprouted up on the Internet, allowing individuals to find a perfect art clip for their email signature. Children could even create their own with ease. Most of the popular email programs allow you to create a signature file that is added to every email message automatically. Creating signature files can be a great classroom activity and is talked about in more detail in the project ideas section of this chapter.

Taking a closer look at the email address from which this message was sent provides us with even more information about the location from which it was sent. When you connect to an Internet server, you choose a username of up to eight alpha-numeric characters. This username is used not only for logging on to your server, but also as part of your email address. Take, for example, Francoise's email address above. Francoise's username is composed of four alpha-numeric digits, "fran". Her email address is therefore a combination of her username and the domain name of her Internet service provider, "somewhere.else.fr". Regardless of the type of address, may it be an email address, a World Wide Web address, or even a computer's domain address such as those talked about in the introduction, the breakdown of the address is similar. Reading from right to left, we can see that "fran@somewhere.else.fr" is the address of a user in France (fr). The network itself is called "else" which is connected to the terminal known as "somewhere". The "at" symbol (@) states that this address is for a user who goes by the username of "fran" at the domain "somewhere.else.fr". Simply put, one's email address is composed of one's username and the domain name of the computer network that supplies the Internet connection.

Using the same right-to-left format, Judy's email address above, "judy@somewhere.com", tells us that the user is on a commercial network (com) known as "somewhere" and the user goes by the user name of "judy". As Judy's address does not end with a two-digit country code, we can assume that her Internet service provider is located in the United States.

Putting Email to Use

Email offers Internet subscribers a wide range of communication possibilities. However, before you can utilize this incredible resource in telecommunications, you need to have first a purpose and second an email address to correspond with. Regarding the classroom, the purpose is clear. From connecting your students to people their own age from around the world and sharing your professional experiences with those across the globe, the country, or your own city to opening up the walls of your classroom to engulf the thoughts, feelings, and emotions of world citizens, email offers limitless possibilities for education, mental and personal growth, and global awareness. Once again, teachers are not faced with answering the question, "Should we put email to use?" but "How do we put email to use?"

I am assuming that you have an Internet account which at the minimum offers you an email address. I am also assuming that you have an email browser. There are as many email browsers as there are service providers. If you are connected to a network at school, chances are that all the Internet software you need is ready to go. If you are connected to the Internet via a dial-up Internet service provider, than your service provider can most likely provide you with a freeware or shareware version of an email browser or recommend one that is best for your type of Internet connection, the type of computer you are using, and your email purpose. If you have the opportunity, you may wish to try out a number of email software programs, keeping in mind the age of your classroom if children will be using the programs themselves. There are also a number of commercial email browsers on the market designed especially for children which you may wish to consider.

Now that you are set with your Internet connection and your email browser, you and a classroom of children sit before a computer screen with no one to communicate with, no letters in your email mailbox, lost in Cyperspace before a voyage ever began. There are many ways to find others in Cyperspace with whom you may wish to correspond, to become keypals with, and to exchange ideas and thoughts with on hundreds of different subjects. Usenet Newsgroups and the World Wide Web are two ways of finding such people, both of which will be discussed in Chapters 3 and 6, but for those of you who wish to get started with email first, or have email-only access, your first step is listservs.

Lists and Listservs

Think of a list as a subscription to a magazine. The magazine is delivered to each subscriber's mailbox regularly. These subscribers all share a common interest in the magazine's subject and content. Turning to the first few pages, one can find letters and articles written by other readers. Deeper into the magazine one finds more in-depth articles, conversations, and interviews. Lists and listservs are very similar only they are electronic, are delivered to your email box, and generally do not have subscription fees. There are as many different lists as there are magazines, each providing subscribers with different content and informational forums. The most powerful element of a list is the ability you have to submit your own views and thoughts. Let's say you were the member of a list on early childhood education. Subscribers to the list email messages discussing early childhood education. These message are in turn electronically forwarded to the email addresses of all subscribers. After reading one letter from a teacher in Nebraska, you decide to respond by emailing a message back to the list, knowing it will then be forwarded to all subscribers. This creates the electronic conversation, the global community communicating with one another regardless of distance and geographic barriers.

Before we dive into the different types of lists and the email addresses that may be of interest to those of us in the educational field, let us first gain some understanding about what a list and a listserv physically are and how they work. A listserv is simply a computer program that maintains email addresses of individuals who have subscribed to the list. Generally the listserv has two addresses, one called the list address and another known as the listserv address. The list address is used when someone wishes to post a message to the list which will be forward to all subscribers. The listserv address accepts commands from people in Cyberspace who wish to subscribe, unsubscribe, or get information about the list. A list, often called a mailing list, can have an open or closed subscription policy, allowing users in Cyberspace to join at will or requiring them to be confirmed by the list owner prior to being added to the list. Likewise, some lists are moderated, meaning that someone reviews all messages posted to the list address before they are sent out to the list subscribers. Other lists are unmoderated, allowing any and all messages posted to be sent to all subscribers automatically.

Let us assume that you want to become a subscriber to the list entitled "Room 13's Question of the Week" (rm13-l), a list that provides an opinion-based question each week for children ages five through fifteen. This question is emailed to all subscribers of the list. List participants respond back to the list sharing their thoughts, opinions, and lives. In order to become a member of this list, you would send an email message to the listserv address, "majordomo@teleport.com". In the body of your email message, you would type "subscribe rm13-l". Listservs often handle commands for many different lists; therefore, every command that you send to a listserv is followed by the name of the list to which you are referring, in this case "rm13-l". Once the message reaches the listserv, your request for a subscription will be processed and your email address will be added to the list. At that point you are a member of the list and any messages sent to the list address, "rm13-l@teleport.com" in this example, will be forwarded to you.

When you become a member of a list, the listserv will reply to your email address with a letter of confirmation. In some cases, this message may instruct you to reply back to the listserv address to reconfirm your subscription. The confirmation message may also contain information about the list to which you have subscribed, such as commands that may be sent to the listserv and the address of the list itself. Most listservs use the same commands that allow users to subscribe and request information about different lists. These commands should always be typed into the body of your email messages and sent to the listserv address. Remember, any message sent to the list's address will be sent to the members of the list, so it is important to send your commands, such as "subscribe rm13-l" to the listserv address.

Below you will find some of the more common listserv commands. In each case "listname" stands for the name of the list that you are seeking information on.

subscribe listname—subscribe to a mailing list

unsubscribe listname—unsubscribe from a mailing list

list—receive a listing of all the mailing lists at a listserv

confirm listname—confirm your subscription to a mailing list

help—return a brief summary of commands from a listserv

info listname—return a help or informational file from a listserv about the specified list

Two of the most helpful listserv commands used by most listservs are "help" and "info". Sending an email message with the word "help" in the body of the message to a listserv address will return to you a help file. This file is in a plain text format and provides you with instructions on how to send commands and what command options the listserv accepts.

The "info" command can also be helpful as it will provide you with an informational file on a specific list. For example, a message to "majordomo @teleport.com", with the command "info rm13-l", will return to your email address a description of the list, the purpose of the list, email addresses used by the list, and often an email address of the owner of the list. In many cases this information file will also provide you with an explanation of the commands accepted by the listserv, in this case, commands accepted by "majordomo@teleport.com".

Listservs can be a very useful tool as they provide us with a wealth of information on an array of subjects. They are easily controlled via email and many are suited not only for teachers, but also for students of all ages. With every listserv, you will find a variety of subscribers with a variety of backgrounds. Lists range from small to enormous, and with the influx of subscribers comes varying degrees of email. Some lists may produce only a couple of messages a week while others email over thirty messages daily. The most proficient way to find the perfect list for your needs is not only to read through Appendix A, Listservs of Interest to Teachers and Students, but also to dial-up your Internet provider, execute your email program, and subscribe.

Finding Listserv Addresses

Thousands of listservs exist, and each day some close down while new ones come alive. There are many ways to discover new listservs that may be of interest to you; however, most of these methods go beyond email capabilities. Following newsgroups on subjects of interest will often produce messages from other newsgroup members; posting a message to a newsgroup asking for information about good listservs is bound to provide you with new lists to check out (see Chapter 3 for further information of Usenet Newsgroups). There also exists a wealth of listserv information available via the World Wide Web (Chapter 6 and Appendix E can provide you with further information on these listserv tools).

Though the information on listservs via newsgroups and the World Wide Web may be the easiest to access, these listserv search tools are of no help to Internet users with email access only. There still exist, however, some basic steps to take to find new lists using email. Take a look at the lists to which you currently subscribe. Using the listserv addresses for those lists, email a message to the listserv with the word "lists" in the body. This command will produce a list of all the lists maintained at that listserv. Often where one list on education will exist, others will as well. This is especially true for lists maintained at university sites whose addresses end in "edu" such as the listserv for Iowa State University, "majordomo@iastate.edu". One can also contact individuals with similar interests via email. Friends are always a source of information, and in the case of the Internet, can be a source of information on lists that are unknown to you.

Finally, one can turn to a mail-order service, which will provide you with an up-to-date list of thousands of active listservs. The "List of Lists Champion" is a for-profit service found on the World Wide Web at "http://users.aol.com/lolchamp/home.htm". Though they charge a fee for their service, they provide an excellent source for finding mailing lists of interest. For more information on the Lists of Lists Champion, email Ken Ramsthaler at "lolchamp@aol.com".

Files, Software, and Pictures via Email

There are many ways to display and download files, software, and pictures over the Internet. However when it comes to email, special preparations have to be taken. Email, as well as Usenet Newsgroups (see Chapter 3), transmit information in ASCII format only, in text characters also known as alpha-numeric characters. Simply put, email can only transmit the symbols found on your keyboard. Some data files, such as documents created by computer applications, software, and pictures are all binary computer files. These files are not in any type of ASCII form and therefore cannot be sent via email without first using an encoding program.

Encoding programs encode binary files into ASCII characters. Once this is done, the file may be sent via email and then decoded back into its original binary form when it has reached its destination. With the help of many encoding/decoding programs, this process is quite simple. Many of the popular email programs, such as the shareware version of Eudora and the commercial version, Eudora Pro, handle this process automatically. These programs allow you to attach a file to a message. As the message is sent, the email program encodes the file. The same is true for receiving binary files, as the message is downloaded from your Internet server, the program decodes the message back into its binary form.

19

In some cases one may need to encode or decode manually and will therefore need a program that can perform this function. These programs are also very easy to handle and are generally point and click on both Windows and Macintosh platforms. (See Appendix C, FTP Sites of Interest to Teachers and Students, to find a shareware version of an encoding/decoding program via the Internet.)

Some listservs also contain files that are retrievable via email. These files are in ASCII format but still require specific listserv commands in order to retrieve them. Take, for example, a listserv known as Galileo. Galileo is list of science lesson plans for teachers. As a member of the list, you receive updates on space exploration as well as the weekly newsletter, Earth and Sky. However, lesson plans will never be emailed directly to you from the list. These lesson plans are archived at the listserv and will be sent to you only if you request them.

In order to retrieve a lesson from the archive we must send email to the listserv making a request for a specific file. Our first task is to get a list of all files found at the Galileo list. To do this we email the Galileo listserv address, "majordomo@unr.edu", with the words "index galileo" in the body of the message. This command will return to our email box a list of all files kept at the listserv for the Galileo list. Look through the list and see if there is a file entitled index. If one exists, this file will most likely contain detailed information about all the other files in the archive. Such a file does exist in the Galileo archive known as "index.all". Sending the command "get galileo index.all" to the listserv address will return the index file to your email box. Scanning this index, we find a file called "erosion.txt". It is described as a lesson on the effects of "erosion by glacier, wind & water." In order to receive this file from the Galileo list, we must send an email message back to the listserv with the words "get galileo erosion.txt". This message tells the listserv, "majordomo@unr.edu", to send the file "erosion.txt" found in the Galileo archives to your email box. Not all lists have files that can be retrieved by email; however, those that do generally work with these "index" and "get" commands. Sending a "help" command to the listserv will often tell you if the listserv accepts these commands.

Professional Listservs

The Internet allows its users to span the globe and bridge geographic boundaries. It allows us to communicate with people in our profession regardless of distance. Many lists exist for the purpose of allowing teachers to communicate with others in their profession and to seek advice, conversation, and professional improvement. Below I have highlighted a few professional lists that I have found useful. However, there are hundreds of other educational lists available to you, some of which are listed in Appendix A.

Edunet

Developed and funded by the Curriculum and Instruction Department of the College of Education at Iowa State University, Edunet is a worldwide email mailing list set up to aid in facilitating educational discussions between teachers and future teachers in the United States and across the globe. Any issue regarding education is appropriate for this list. Edunet is a great professional resource for those of us seeking answers to educational questions or simply searching for educational conversation on pedagogy, theory, practice, or classroom situations.

edunet@iastate.edu (list address)

majordomo@iastate.edu (listserv address)

Galileo

As mentioned above, Galileo is a space and science list for educators. List owner Bill Protz provides subscribers with a weekly newsletter from the Earth and Sky radio show, occasional updates on various space shuttle and other space-related events, as well as conversations relating to science education from Galileo list subscribers. Galileo also maintains a science lesson archive. These lesson files are retrievable via email by using the command "get galileo index.all". This command will result in an index list of lesson plans sent back to you from the listserv. For more information on the

Galileo list, send email to "majordomo@unr.edu" with "info galileo" in the body of the message.

galileo@unr.edu (list address)

majordomo@unr.edu (listserv address)

Novae Group Teachers Networking for the Future

The Novae list is very helpful for teachers who work with technology in their professional lives and their classrooms. Each week Novae sends out a newsletter to all subscribers. This newsletter contains addresses for WWW sites that would be of interest not only to teachers, but also to students. The newsletter gives you weekly information on educational programs on the Internet as well as new ideas for Internet use in the classroom.

novae@idbsu.idbsu.edu (list address)

listserv@idbsu.idbsu.edu(listserv address)

Teachers Applying Whole Language (TAWL)

The TAWL list is similar in its format to Edunet. It is a list of teachers and future teachers conversing on various issues dealing with the application of Whole Language in the classroom. From spelling, reading, and writing to the theory behind whole language, the TAWL list can be a helpful and informative teacher resource. Once you are a member, replies and questions of your own can be emailed to the list address. As this list has literally hundreds of members, it does not take long before someone replies to your post, opening dialogue and global conversation.

tawl@listserv.arizona.edu (list address)

listserv@listserv.arizona.edu (listserv address)

Today in History

Ever wonder what happened today in history or whose birthday it is? Well, members of this list can tell you. As a subscriber, you will receive a daily note on the history of that day. Each message is packed with history facts, celebrations, and birthdays. Sharing these messages with your students can open up many avenues for further study and exploration. Printing each message on paper and putting these pages in a folder is a great way for children of all ages to take interest in history. I have a folder filled with this information sitting on the shelf in my classroom. Children freely browse through it, discovering history facts and searching for people in history who share their birth date. In some cases, Today in History sparks the interest of a child or a classroom, allowing for further investigation and historical study.

today@pobox.com(list address)

majordomo@pobox.com (listserv address)

Classroom Project Ideas

Keypals Through the International Email Classroom Connection (IECC)

Classroom keypal projects are a great way to get a whole classroom involved with the Internet. Keypals not only demonstrate the efficiency of the Internet to children, they also allow students to work on their writing and personal skills as they communicate with others from around the world. Finding keypals through email access would be challenging without the help of the International Email Classroom Connection (IECC) list. This list makes getting a classroom keypal situation setup as easy as sending an email message. Once you have subscribed to the list address, you are sent instructions on how to submit for classroom keypals. By simply filling out a provided form and sending it back to the list, your search for a group of children from somewhere in the world is under way. You can also read keypal requests from other list members.

I have been using keypals through the Internet for the past two years and have found that the children gain many skills from such a project. In my classroom, where I have twenty-eight students and three computers, we first respond to our keypal letters on paper. Once these letters are edited, students take turns typing them into the computer. When all letters have been entered and copied to a single file, they are emailed to our corresponding classroom. This experience has given my students—from a Portland, Oregon, inner-city school—the chance to write and become friends with people their own age from a private school on the east coast of the United States. Students have gained not only friendships, but also writing and communication skills while they continue to develop their typing skills and experiences with technology.

IECC has subscribers from all over the world and is not limited to keypals in the United States.

iecc@stolaf.edu (list address)

iecc-request@stolaf.edu (listserv address)

Kid Conversations: On-line Conversation Lists

It is a proven fact that children love to talk, especially to each other. One of the best ways to encourage appropriate conversation in the classroom is through various lists set up for the purpose of kids talking to kids. KidCafe and Kidzmail are two such lists intended to facilitate conversation between school-aged children throughout the world. Imagine a new, independent work station in your classroom devoted to responding and communicating with others from around the world. These lists can provide just that, a place for children to talk with others their own age with different thoughts, experiences, and cultural backgrounds. By simply subscribing to one of these lists, messages will be sent to your email box. Children working at the "Internet" station can practice their communication and technology skills by reading and responding to these email messages. If Internet is not an option in the classroom and you are using a form of the "Sneaker-Net" method that I spoke about in the introduction, then these lists can still be beneficial to your students. One option is to print the letters that have been sent from the list and have students respond on paper or on disk. It may not allow for the direct Internet connectivity, but it does allow for the global technology experience through communications and word-processing skills.

For the list addresses and listserv addresses of KidCafe, Kidzmail, and other kid-forum lists, see the "Kids" section in Appendix A, List-servs of Interest to Teachers and Students.

Room 13's Question of the Week

Lists that encourage child conversation on line do have their limitations with regard to whole classroom situations. It has been my experience that students generally work independently or in small groups responding and conversing with other subscribers. It is often difficult and sometimes not feasible to maintain whole class interaction on such lists. It is for that reason that in January, 1996, I began "The Room 13's Question of the Week" list (RM13-L). RM13-L was established for the purpose of inviting conversation between classrooms and students ages five through fifteen across the world. Each Friday, students from Room 13 at Sitton Elementary School in Portland, Oregon, vote on a topic question. This question is in the form of a single sentence, such as "Would you rather fly like a bird or swim like a fish?" (the first question ever posted to the list).

Members of the list are encouraged to answer the question by replying back to the list. The difference between this list and other child-centered discussion lists is that RM13-L provides short, single-sentence, opinion-based questions that whole classrooms can easily respond to and discuss. Students or classrooms also have the option of recommending their own question for the week. As the list grows in subscriptions, I see future plans to include graphing, charting, and analyzing the data that any subscriber to RM13-L receives, thereby fully integrating this listserv project into the curriculum.

rm13-l@teleport.com(list address)

majordomo@teleport.com (listserv address)

rm13-l-request@teleport.com(Kevin Crotchett, owner)

Emotion Smilies		Character Smilies	
|>@	Sleepy by Alyssa Hagen	_B-)	Scuba Diver by Joseph Lance
#:-D	Ahh! by Ben Nead	{:^)	King with his crown by Ben Nead
<:-)	Happy boy by Michael Dyuck	<:^[	Mad Scientist by Michael Dyuck
=:-)	Sad Bill by Chris McKinney	~:~)	Baby Hewy by Joseph Letcher
=:>o	Shocked by Kendra Rheault	[:|]	Robot by Lauren Hurley
|:-}	Happy with Tongue out by Lauren Hurley	=}>	Le Monsieur by Lauren Hurley
;<?	Duh! by Lauren Hurley	*<:{}	Wizard by Jessie Mills
<|:-o	Surprised by Joseph Percell	8+|	Crash Dummy by Jarrid Ybarra
%^)	Wacko by Mehgan Schmitt	?:O	Elvis by Lauren Hurley

FIG. 2–1: *Smilies by Room 13*

Adding That Human Touch: Smilies and Email Signatures

Whether we are studying the expanse of North America, involved in creative writing, using and practicing the multiplication tables, or discussing the aesthetic characteristics of the *Mona Lisa*, children are bound to be doodling on something. Writing funny sayings; drawing strange symbols, animals, and faces; or just making designs on a scrap piece of paper, their folders, or, yes it happens, their desks, children (and adults) love to create. It is often believed that email, made up of electronic impulses and text, takes away from one's graphic creativity. The fact is that it can enhance and challenge creative energies. Smilies and email signatures are two electronic mediums that allow us to create pictures through text characters.

Smilies, also known as emoticons, are smiles and frowns that can easily be placed in an email message. The most generic of these smilies are the smile, :), the frown :(, and the winking smile, ;). As you can see, these smilies are made up from colons, parentheses, and semicolons. If you are still having a difficult time seeing the smiles and frowns, try turning the page ninety degrees to the right!

One classroom activity that my students have found to be very enjoyable is creating smilies. After giving students a paper copy of a keyboard and showing them the three basic smilies above, the class discussed other keys that could be used in creating new emoticons. We then went to work, creating and enjoying our time as we developed new ways to express ourselves in our email messages. From the sleepy smilie by Alyssa to Wacko by Meghan, students turned from representing emotions with their smilies to building character portraits such as the scuba diver by Joe and the portrait of Elvis by Lauren (see Fig. 2–1). The creation of smilies was successful for all levels and began to appear in my students' email messages immediately after the exercise. The smilies brought emotion, life, and laughter into the cold print of their email and proved to be a successful art and technology lesson for all.

Signatures, as mentioned in the beginning of this chapter, are another way to express creativity and personality in a world of text. Email signatures are added to the bottom of email messages. They generally provide you with some basic information, such as the sender's name, snail mail address (postal address), and Internet addresses. Often, especially in the case of children, these signatures contain art made from text symbols known as ASCII art. Using quarter-inch grid paper and a paper copy of a keyboard, my classroom again went to work creating and personalizing our email messages. After taking a brief look at some ASCII art examples similar to those found on Francoise's signature and discussing the text keys used to create them, students went to work creating their own ASCII art. The grid paper helped to keep text symbols in line and the picture clear, making it easier to transfer their art from paper to computer. These ASCII art creations were later used to create email signatures which were used by the students on their email messages (see Fig. 2–2).

Smilies and signatures allow us to personalize our email and to show emotion in an otherwise emotionless medium—print. They

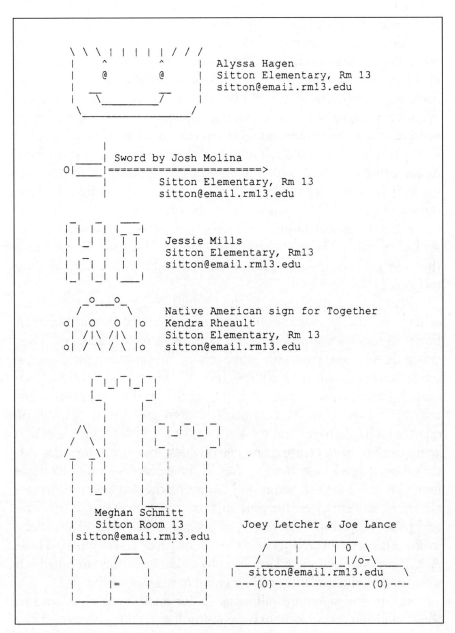

FIG. 2–2:   *ASCII Art Creation and Room 13 Signatures*

demonstrate that even technology and email can be creative and graphically interesting. They bring out laughter and human expression as students create and share their art with their friends in their own classroom and on the Internet.

Surveys and Data Studies

Surveys and data studies offer any classroom the chance to collect, analyze, and work with data across the curriculum. From surveying classmates' thoughts about a current classroom novel to collecting data on the number of pets in first graders' homes to gathering data on the phases of the moon, the process of surveying and data collection is a fantastic multipurpose educational tool. This process is only enhanced with email access through the Internet. Students interested in topics that require some surveying can easily invite such data to their email box by posting survey questions to selected lists. Take, for example, a posting found on the list, Kidzmail from Derek Young, a fifth grader from Lewisville, Texas (see Fig. 2–3). This message is the perfect example of email's educational potential. Derek utilized email and mailing lists to conduct an in-depth data study, not only gathering data for his science project, but also gaining essential technology skills. By posting his message to email mailing lists that allow for student conversations, such as Kidzmail and KidCafe, Derek received completed surveys from throughout the United States and the world. Through the use of digital technology, email, and the Internet, Derek's survey and data study went far beyond the walls of his classroom or his middle school.

Email and listservs provide Internet users with a large variety of information and services. For education, listservs allow us and our students to connect with the world in a timely manner. They provide us with near-immediate feedback, crossing all geographic barriers, allowing us to further our communication and technology skills. Lists can be easily set up for individual and/or whole class interaction. From keypals to conversational lists, children interact with others from all over the globe, an interaction that could not easily take place without the Internet. With lists such as RM13-L, Mathmagic,

```
Return-Path: owner-kidzmail@asuvm.inre.asu.edu
Date:      Fri, 19 Jan 1996 09:44:22 CST
Reply-To: "Kidzmail:  Kids Exploring Issues And Interests
           Electronically" <kidzmail@asuvm.inre.asu.edu>
Sender:    "Kidzmail:  Kids Exploring Issues And Interests
           Electronically" <kidzmail@asuvm.inre.asu.edu>
From:      Connie <ds_maxwell@venus.twu.edu>
Subject:   Help--Science Project

To: Multiple recipients of list KIDZMAIL <KIDZMAIL@ASUVM.INRE.ASU.EDU>

My name is Derek Young. I am a 5th grader at Degan Elementary in Lewisville,
TX. For my Science Fair Project I am trying to prove that kids who eat healthy
meals don't get sick very often. I would appreciate your help.
  PLEASE complete my questionaire and send it to DS_Maxwell@TWU.EDU.

Each day we need:

Bread Group - (bread, cereal, rice and pasta)  9 servings
Vegetable Group - 4 servings
Fruit Group - ( fruit or juice)  3 servings
Milk Group - (milk, yogurt and cheese)  2-3 servings
Meat Group - (meat, chicken, fish, beans, eggs, nuts and peanut butter -
  2 servings

DO YOU EAT HEALTHY??   __never  __sometimes __usually  __always


HOW MANY DAYS HAVE YOU MISSED SCHOOL (BECAUSE YOU WERE SICK)
THIS YEAR??
  __none  __1-2 days  __3-5 days  __more than 5 days.

Results from my survey will be posted to this list. If you know of other lists
I might write to I would appreciate your help.

THANKS,
Derek
```

FIG. 2–3: *Email from Derek*

and Family Math (see Appendix A), classrooms can integrate email and lists into the daily curriculum, demystifying technology and education by demonstrating a connection between daily lessons, real-world technology, and the academic routine.

THREE

Usenet Newsgroups:
The Electronic Newspaper

Imagine bringing into your classroom a newspaper that contains articles on politics, business, education, community resources, entertainment, hobbies, and sports, a newspaper that contains articles, editorials, and reader responses. As you turn the page to read on, a new article appears right before your eyes, which in turn creates a conversation of replies that develops into another whole newspaper. This is exactly what is happening on Usenet Newsgroups. Literally thousands of subjects are being discussed, some moderated and others left to their own demise. Topics range from environmental issues in "alt.save.the.earth" to political issues in "bit.listserv.politics" to educational subjects such as those found in "alt.education.alternative" or "k12.lang.arts" to recreational subjects in "rec.suba" and local issues in "pdx.forsale" or "pdx.education" (two local groups carried in Portland, Oregon). Newsgroups read like a newspaper, but are unlike any paper found on the newsstand, for newsgroups allow for response, discussion, controversy, and worldwide interaction.

In many ways, newsgroups are similar to listservs (see Chapter 2). Individuals participating in the group focus their energy on one particular subject. As participants read and respond to the newsgroup posts, the electronic conversation is created. However, with newsgroups, participants are able to sort through the articles and read only those of interest to them, whereas with a listserv, each and every article is emailed to you regardless of your interest in that article.

Usenet History

Newsgroups found their start in North Carolina in the early eighties. College students discovered a method to transmit text from one UNIX machine to another. A few dozen articles were transmitted daily over phone lines. Over the next few years, with the help and interest of universities and software companies, this early form of Usenet Newsgroups spread to a couple hundred sites that were sending and receiving a few thousand messages a day at much greater speeds. It was at this same time that the Internet's potential was being realized, and with the help from the NSFnet, newsgroups began to utilize Internet technology and infrastructure. Newsgroups went away from the classic telephone-line transfer and began to use the NSFnet as a method of moving data from one Usenet site to the next.

Today, Usenet sites covering thousands of topics can be found throughout the world. The newsgroups offered to you depend on your Internet server and your location. Many newsgroups, such as the "alt" category, are carried throughout the world; however, many local agencies, institutions, and regions have created their own set of newsgroups that are of interest only to those in the geographic region. In Portland, Oregon, for example, there is an array of newsgroups beginning with "pdx". These groups deal primarily with Portland issues and are not of interest to the carriers and newsgroup readers in Miami. They are therefore not transmitted to, nor picked up by, the servers outside the northwestern region of the United States.

Graphics and Usenet Newsgroups

Newsgroups can also be the cause of great controversy. Originally, newsgroups could only transmit text, also known as ASCII, and though this remains true today, graphic images can also be sent with the help of encoding/decoding programs. This technology has spurred on the growth of whole subcategory of newsgroups devoted to computer images, "the alt.binary . . ." groups. Though some such as "alt.binaries.pictures.misc", are very innocent, these groups are mostly filled with erotic material and should be avoided in the classroom situation. But for those activities and projects that do require sending binary images via email and newsgroups, one will have to learn to utilize an encoding/decoding program. These programs encode binary files into ASCII format, which can then be posted to a newsgroup or emailed. Once received, the reader must decode the ASCII file back into a binary file, and hence a graphic image or software program. There are many encoding and decoding programs available on the Internet for every type of computer. (Turn to Chapter 5 and Appendix C, on File Transfer Protocol (FTP), to find some useful sites to begin your search for an encoding/decoding program.)

In order to read Usenet Newsgroups, you will need to obtain one of the various newsgroup reader programs which can be found on the Internet. There are many different programs for each platform. It is useful to experiment with more than one program to find the one that best fits your personality and needs. Note that while some of the software available from the Internet is "FreeWare," meaning you need not pay for it, much of the software is "ShareWare," and gives you the permission to try it out for up to 30 days. After the trial period is over, the user is required by copyright to pay for the product, generally by way of a land mail address given with the program. Many of these newsgroups readers also contain encoding and decoding capabilities. This makes encoding and decoding easy, as the program encodes or decodes binary files when they are sent or received.

Getting to Know a Group Before
Introducing It to the Classroom

Once you have chosen a newsgroup reader, it is important to become familiar with the newsgroups that you will be using in the classroom. Many newsgroups are moderated by someone in Cyberspace. This person guides conversation and takes action against those individuals who may be violating the rules of the newsgroups. Moderated groups, as well as some unmoderated groups, publish a most Frequently Asked Question (FAQ) document which is posted to the newsgroup on a regular basis. This document contains information about the newsgroup's purpose and guidelines to the general subject matter. The FAQ is a great way to get to know a newsgroup and to judge its content appropriateness for your students' age group and needs. Reviewing the FAQ and reading some posts over a period of time will give you a strong impression of the group's general attitude, style, and acceptance of newcomers.

In many ways each newsgroup is not unlike a neighborhood. Some are very open and welcoming, while others may be reluctant to accept newcomers. Some community members are gracious, polite, and kind, while others are less tolerant to opposing viewpoints. In short, newsgroups are Cyberspace communities, some with many members, others with very few. Some newsgroup communities are very migrant, while others have the solid base of lifers. Browsing a group prior to introducing it to a classroom will prepare you for working with the group—interacting, conversing, and sharing the experience with your students. It will also give you a sense of the proper etiquette used when conversing with that group.

Once you have become familiar with a newsgroup, it is a good idea to become a member of the group by writing an introductory post and interacting with other readers. Remember, a newsgroup is a Cyberspace community, and if you and your class wish to interact with that community, you need to become a part of the community. Let them know that you are out there in the depths of Cyberspace just hanging out and listening in. As time passes and you begin to become familiar with the group, engage yourself in the discussions and familiarize yourself with the regular members. These members may become a great resource to you as you begin a class project involving the newsgroup. One might also consider telling the group about the students who will be involved in the newsgroup project. Some members may greatly appreciate knowing about a classroom that is part of their newsgroup, others may not care, but the information is always nice to have.

Finding That Perfect Newsgroup

There are over 13,000 newsgroups on Usenet at any given time. That's over 13,000 communities to become a part of, and new ones are being developed each day. With such a wide selection it is often difficult to find the perfect group for your classroom needs. It helps to understand a little about the names given to newsgroups to judge their usefulness. Newsgroup names are made up of a series of words and abbreviations hooked together with periods (.). The first abbreviation will tell you about the category the group is in. This is a general category heading and deals more with the type of individual likely to be participating in the group and less with the actual topic of the group. Following this abbreviation is a series of descriptive words that aim to describe the group as much as possible. For example, one can find many education newsgroups in the alternative category, such as "alt.education.elementary" which deals with general elementary education. The "alt." category is by far the largest, with groups discussing politics, education, computers, games, humor, kids, graphic images, shareware, and so on. Other categories are more defined, such as the "k12." series of newsgroups dealing with all types of issues in k12 education. There is also a "rec." category for recreation, "comp." for computer related groups, "clari." for news media information, and "bit." categories which follow a few listservs in newsgroup format, just to name a few. Other categories relate to the language being spoken or geographic region that the group deals with. For example, the "de." category is written in Dutch while "uk." categories are about the United Kingdom and "fj." are about Fiji. Finally, there exist the local area newsgroups which are generally not carried nor picked up too far from the original location. The "pdx." groups in Portland, Oregon or the "wil." groups found at Willamette University are two examples of local newsgroup categories.

Once one is familiar with newsgroup names and hierarchy, it is easier to decipher the subject matter, but some confusion can still arise if one is searching for a group on a very specific subject. If a student was interested in polling dirt bike enthusiasts about their favorite dirt bike manufacturer, then graphing and comparing the information, it could take that student days to search through a list of over 13,000 newsgroups to find one that suits her needs. Even if she searchs only the "alt." and "rec." categories, the task could be overwhelming and time-consuming. There may also exist some dirt bike groups in other categories, resulting in the student's getting an incomplete data base. It is from this frustration and confusion of newsgroup titles and subjects that people in Cyberspace have created searchable newsgroup indexes. Using your favorite World Wide Web browser (discussed in Chapter 6) go to "http://www.cen.uivc.edu/cgi-bin/find-news". Once connected, input a single subject and in moments you will receive a nearly complete list of current newsgroups discussing that subject. Again it is important to note that the resulting list may contain newsgroups that are not intended for all audiences.

Classroom Projects

Keypals

One of the easiest ways to integrate Usenet Newsgroups into the classroom's daily routine is with keypals. Students can become familiar with the workings of Usenet Newsgroups by browsing through "k12.chat.elementary", "k12.chat.junior", or "k12.chat.senior". These groups are filled with requests from other students from around the United States and other countries who are seeking keypals, an electronic variation of the penpal. Students can browse the entries to find another person of the same age with similar interests. Students may also decide to post their own messages, asking for others to write back via an email address. Within days, one can guarantee a couple of replies at a minimum.

Once a keypal is set up and correspondence has begun between the two students, other opportunities may arise. Sharing class work and exchanging biographies, stories, and lists of favorite hobbies can be developed naturally during an in-class writing time, then emailed to a keypal or posted to a newsgroup. Geography and cultural studies are also natural extensions from Internet-oriented projects. Keypals can be marked on a map and their region and culture studied. This new knowledge can then be easily shared with the class and the student's keypal, showing them their interest in their culture and life.

The most incredible advantage of keypals and "newsgroup chat" is the ability they have to shrink the world into a small community. As one fourth grader stated, "It is so weird that Zara (from Singapore) likes the same things as I do. She already wrote back to me and I just emailed her yesterday. I thought it would take at least a week to hear from the other side of the world!" Usenet allows for a quick response time and near-immediate feedback, accelerating a child's learning and interest while bridging global gaps and cultural differences.

Newsgroup Surveys

One question that often arises with regard to the Internet and classroom use is in the primary classroom. Even the youngest elementary students can become familiar with the Internet. The World Wide Web, discussed in Chapter 6, is one way to engage the six-year-old with visual and audio effects, but it can lack the personal interaction that makes the global community such a powerful tool. One way to enhance Internet interaction in the primary classroom and throughout the grades is through newsgroup surveys. Many primary classes work with a curriculum that deals with the community, people, and cultures around them. This often inspires surveys done by primary students on opinions about sports or weather, for example. On any given day you will likely find a clipboard-carrying five-year-old walking the halls of my school asking adults whether they prefer rain or snow. This survey information is then brought back to the kindergarten classroom and shared with members of the class in the form of a very basic data study.

Newsgroups can be used in the same manner. Younger students can formulate a survey question that interests them while at the same time think about questions that would interest others from many different parts of the state, country, and the world. After selecting the appropriate newsgroup, such as "k12.elementary.chat" for elementary students or "clari.news.weather" or a local weather newsgroup for the weather enthusiast, the question can be posted to the group, asking for replies to be either emailed to the classroom or posted back to the newsgroup. Over the next few days replies will be coming in, many or few, depending on the newsgroup. Replies can be then recorded, charted, and mapped. Writing skills can be practiced by writing thank-you notes and emailing them to respondents, thus increasing a student's email experiences. Survey data and findings can be looked at on a local, state, or global level, all depending on the question posted and the newsgroup it was posted to.

The natural extension of surveying into the upper grades is also a great way to introduce students to the uses of Usenet. As a whole class or small group, students can survey and poll others their age or target a specific group of people, as well as a specific area of the world. Students work through the scientific process, formulating a question, writing a hypothesis, gathering and analyzing data, and proposing a conclusion. The results of the survey can then be shared with the class, the survey respondents, and the newsgroup.

Ask the Experts

Not a single week goes by in the life of a teacher that a question asked by students cannot be completely answered. The Internet is one resource that can be employed to find an answer. A student may be directed to the computer to conduct a quick newsgroup search on the subject. Once one or more applicable newsgroups are found, the student can post the question to the newsgroup(s). In the days to come, it becomes part of that student's responsibility to read those newsgroups or check email for a reply and to follow up with necessary thank-yous. Any answers to the proposed question are then shared with the class. This process puts the investigative responsibility into the hands of the learner, helping to make the student in charge of his own learning and demystifying the learning process.

Teacher Chat and Support

Educators may find that newsgroups help to break down feelings of isolation. Keypals for teachers and newsgroup chat can be found in "k12.teacher.chat", with basic conversation between teachers. More subject-oriented discussions can be found as well. From language arts to mathematics, you can find teachers talking about their profession throughout the k12 newsgroup category (see Appendix B). Participation in these newsgroups helps to open up lines of communication with other teachers throughout the state, the country, and the world who are experiencing similar issues. This is also a great place to turn for help and advice from other professionals. Bored with the same science lesson on plants? Ask other teachers of your grade level from around the world for more ideas in "k12.teacher.chat" or "k12.science", or turn to the general community in "sci.bio.botany".

Newsgroup Authors

Imagine a publisher willing to publish any story or poem and distribute that story or poem to the world, free of charge—as long as it was written by a student. There is such a publisher who can be found in Usenet. "Schl.proj.writing" and "schl.stu.author" are two groups that have been created for the purpose of publishing students' stories, poems, and articles. Publishing student work to these newsgroups can be a great way for students and teachers to become familiar with the use of Usenet. Usenet publishing can be easily integrated into writing activities and existing classroom curriculum as it does not require whole class involvement. If the "schl." category is not available to you through your current Internet server, do not despair. It is not uncommon to find student-published writings in many of the student chat groups such as "k12.chat.elementary", "schl.stu.high", and "schl.stu.hobbies".

In My Opinion!

Student opinions about the *Mona Lisa*, the current political race, the morals of wars in history, or which toothpaste tastes best are all conversations I have heard in classrooms—conversations where engaged students presented their opinions and backed them up with factual support or personal belief statements. Conversations in the form of a friendly debate occur all the time on the Internet in many groups throughout Usenet. It is a great medium to invite opinion into the classroom from people outside your local area, state, or country. Through a basic student chat group, one class polled other students from Australia during a U.S. presidential election to gain insight on worldwide opinion. A second-grade classroom opened up a forum on the best-tasting toothpaste in another chat group. In each case, students were learning to express themselves as individuals with opinions and preferences, learning to formulate those opinions into conversation.

The ability to formulate a personal opinion is possibly one of the most important characteristics of adult culture. With selected newsgroups, one can carry these conversations into Cyperspace, gaining new and completely different perspectives on the subject. In "misc.kids.consumers", children as well as adults are able to discuss toys and other kid products—a subject children definitely have opinions about.

Project Channels

The k12 category also has a series of groups known as "k12.channel (0–12)". These 13 channels are specifically designed for large classroom or whole school projects. They can be used by anyone who wishes to apply for a channel for up to two months. The projects themselves are ones that require telecommunications and cannot be completed through any other newsgroup.

For the beginner, the best use of these groups is to monitor the projects and perhaps participate in those relevant to the classroom situation. It is important to note that there are two different structures the channels may take. Some channel projects are open, asking anyone interested to join, while other channel projects may be closed. A closed channel is set up for only certain individuals to participate in, such as high school science instructors or seventh-grade earth science students. Anyone is free to monitor and follow closed projects, but only those specified are asked to participate.

Teachers or students interested in applying for a channel may do so by sending for information via email to "helen@k12.oit.umass. edu", or one could monitor the newsgroup" k12.projects" for more information from the k12 project coordinator. Similar to the k12 project channels, write to "info@acme.fred.org" for information regarding the "schl.proj.channel(1–4)" newsgroups.

As you become more familiar with Usenet Newsgroups offered by your Internet server, you are bound to find other newsgroups that are of interest to your classroom. Educational newsgroups constitute a very small portion of the thousands of newsgroups floating through Cyberspace. It is important not to forget about other groups that may be equally valuable to a specific classroom situation or project.

Usenet Newsgroups are a very powerful part of the Internet. They bring the world into the classroom, and with that world comes a few thousand different communities. Newsgroups allow us and our students to explore and learn through the written word, gaining from those words new insights, viewpoints, opinions, acquaintances, and friends. Newsgroups break the world down and squeeze it into an electronic impulse, an electronic community that reminds us of our connections and our similarities as the citizens of the global community.

FOUR

File Transfer Protocol: Millions of Computers at Your Fingertips

"How many people remember the math concepts that we were introduced to yesterday? Good, well today we are going to continue to look at multiplication through our math stations. But before we dive into our math stations, I want to point out the two new programs that are running on the computers. You will all have a chance to spend fifteen minutes on each program over the next few days during our math exploration time. They are both shareware and we need to decide which one to purchase; we can only afford one. When you are at that station, you are to experiment with the two programs and complete one of our classroom software recommendation forms. Any questions?"

Imagine being able to explore a math concept with your children that included trial software. Software that could be previewed by teachers and students prior to purchasing. In today's national funding crisis, previewing software is essential to schools. The Internet and File Transfer Protocol (FTP) allow you and your students to download thousands of shareware software. These programs, many which are as complex in nature as some well-known commercial programs, operate under the shareware idea, that is, you have a thirty-day trial period to test out the program prior to purchasing it. Should you and your students decide that the program is useful, you are required by copyright laws to send payment to the author or the company of the software for use of the program beyond the thirty-day trial period.

What Is FTP and How Does It Work?

FTP is one of the oldest protocols of the Internet. As mentioned in the introduction to this book, the Internet got its start back in 1969. This is also when the concept of FTP began. In the late sixties, college students and scientists experimented with transferring articles and text documents between two distant, connected computers. This research led to the development of the TCP Internet protocol, which in turn allowed many computers to access information across greater distances simultaneously. Soon, text-based transfers moved to what is known today as email, while binary, or computer programs continued to rely on a File Transfer Protocol method; hence the name FTP.

Like email, Gopher, and the World Wide Web, File Transfer Protocol (FTP) is an Internet protocol by which one computer can be connected to another in order to transfer and share data. This connection is made via the FTP address. For example, if you wanted to email someone, you would have to know their email address. If you wished to access an FTP site and download a copy of a shareware math game, then you would need to know the FTP address.

FTP addresses resemble many other Internet addresses. While email addresses contain the @ sign, signifying the system the user is on, FTP addresses are separated by periods. For example, a popular FTP site known as the Coast to Coast Software Repository has an FTP address of "ftp.coast.net". This FTP site contains shareware covering hundreds of subjects. In order to access this site, you would first connect to your Internet service. Then using FTP software (often provided to you by your Internet server), you could access the Coast to Coast Software Repository in Clarkston, Minnesota. Once you are connected, the Coast to Coast system will request a login. Coast to Coast is one of thousands of anonymous FTP sites, thus at the login you simply type the word, "anonymous" and press enter. The system will then prompt you for a password. The rule of thumb for anonymous FTP servers is that you use your email address as the password. It is that simple.

I have mentioned the general breakdown of Internet addresses and how this can often give us reference to the type of system the computer is on and the physical location of the computer system. In this case, the Coast to Coast address, "ftp.coast.net", tells us only that the system we are accessing is on a large network (net). There is no reference to the location of the FTP site found within the FTP address. As physical creatures, we tend to be fixated on space, time, and location. The Internet, however, is electronic. Therefore you may travel across the country or across the globe without ever being aware of your location. Other FTP addresses that you may come in contact with, such as "oak.oakland.edu", another popular FTP site, do give us a number of clues as to the location and the organization. From the "edu" portion of the address we know that the system is from an education facility, known by the Internet as "oakland" and on the computer "oak". From this information we can make an educated guess that we would be connected to a FTP site located in Rochester, Michigan, home of Oakland University, or perhaps an educational campus in Oakland, California. In this case the former is true.

Accessing and Downloading Files and Software

As the Internet has grown, FTP has become a highly useful tool for transferring computer software, binary programs and files, and large text documents. Today, FTP is still a frequently used protocol. In fact, many Internet users access FTP sites without ever knowing it, through their World Wide Web browser (see Chapter 6 for more information on accessing FTP through your Web browser). FTP is not only used throughout the Internet community to transfer software, but it is highly useful as a means to transfer very large text documents, such as the transcript to Martin Luther King Jr.'s "I have a dream" speech.

Imagine for a moment that you have a friend who is also a teacher and who lives across the country. While reading the latest email message from her, you become interested in a lesson that she is teaching on the water cycle. More important, you could really use that lesson this week. Emailing her back, you find out that the lesson includes a basic water program for the computer, a program that one of her parents wrote that allows the students to experiment with the effects mountain ranges can have on the water cycle. She emails you a copy of the lesson plan and tells you to FTP to "teach.lesson.edu" and download a copy of the water program from the "/pub/lessons/ k12/water" directory. She explains that the program is simply too large to encode into text (see Chapter 2 for more information on encoding) and send it through email, so she has left a copy of the program on a computer site that you can access via anonymous FTP. Great. Now all you have to do is figure out how to use that FTP program.

It is actually very easy. If you are using a Windows- or Macintosh-based system, the process is only a series of points and clicks with the mouse. In the case that you are using a UNIX-based system, FTP is accessed through a series of commands. The type of software and FTP system you use will depend on your Internet connection and service provider.

To utilize the FTP protocol and to retrieve the documents and programs stored on other computers, you will of course need FTP software. This software, found on the Net and through your Internet provider (see Appendix C), will allow you to enter the FTP address. Once you have connected to the remote computer and entered in the anonymous login and your email address for a password, you will be able to maneuver through the remote computer's directories. In the example above, your friend left the water program on a computer with the FTP address of "teach.lesson.edu". In order to retrieve the water program, you would connect to the remote computer by using the FTP address. Once connected, you would move to the desired directory. The method by which you move through the directories on a remote system will of course depend on the FTP software you are using and the computer platform you are on. Understanding your FTP software is no different than understanding your word processor—fluency comes with familiarity and practice.

Once you have located the "pub" directory, change to the "lessons" directory, then to the "k12" directory where you will find the "water" directory. It is in this directory that you should be able to find the desired water program your friend mentioned. To make the directory structure of a computer more understandable, think of it like a filing cabinet. Logging on to the computer system is like unlocking the cabinet and opening the top drawer. Once inside this top drawer, you are presented with folders. Among these folders you would find one entitled "pub". Inside that folder, or directory, is a folder called "lesson" which contains still more folders. A directory system on a computer is structured in the same fashion as the folders in the filing cabinet. Each directory can contain files or more directories, which in turn may contain files and/or more directories.

Classroom Uses of FTP

As mentioned above, FTP allows you to obtain computer programs and large text documents. While this is not likely to become a largely used protocol by the average Internet user, it can at times be very helpful. The two uses of FTP that I have already mentioned—retrieving unabridged copies of famous speeches or previewing computer software—are two uses that I have found to be very helpful for my fifth graders.

Historical Speeches

Be it the birthday of J.F. Kennedy or a unit on civil rights, FTP can bring to the classroom a library of enrichment. From President Kennedy's speech of the first man on the moon to Martin Luther King Jr.'s "I have a dream" speech, FTP can deliver unabridged copies to the classroom, allowing them to be read, reviewed, analyzed, and studied in detail. By logging on to the FTP site "ftp. msstate.edu" and moving to the "pub/docs/history" directory, you will find literally hundreds of speeches and text-based documents at your fingertips. Whether you are looking for a printed copy of the U.S. constitution, a transcript of the Japanese surrender during World War II, or one of many other nationally and internationally known speeches, this site is here to help.

Previewing Shareware Software in the Classroom

In the beginning of this chapter, I described a situation from my classroom where students were to experiment with new computer software, record their opinions, and make purchase recommendations. This process was made possible by the Internet and FTP. After the introduction of a multiplication unit, I connected to the Internet and went on a search for computer programs written for elementary students on multiplication. In order to do this, I of course needed to know some FTP addresses to search. These addresses, obtained by reading newsgroups, listservs, and Web search engines (see Chapter 6), are known to contain shareware computer programs of all types, and from my previous visits to these sites, I know that they contain computer software related to education (see Appendix C).

I started my search at the Coast to Coast Software Repository. Once connected to their FTP site, "ftp.coast.net", I looked into the directory known as "SimTel". It is in this directory that shareware software can be found by category. From this directory I shifted to the "msdos" directory, as my classroom has MS DOS computers. Contained here, I found a list of categories. Each category is a directory itself, containing the actual shareware software programs. I quickly found a directory known as "educate". Once inside that directory, a large list of computer programs can be found, all dealing with education in one form or another. At the top of this list is a file entitled "00index.txt". Nearly all FTP directories that you encounter have an index file. This is a text file which contains information on the contents of the directory, the names of programs found within, and a brief description of each. After downloading the index file and reading it through a text editor or a word processor, I found a program called "amd30.zip". According to the description, this program is a shareware of animated multiplication and division games for children, perfect for my current math unit and my classroom.

Notice that the program ends in the suffix "zip". This tells us that the program is compressed using the zip format. In order to use the program for my classroom, it will first have to be decompressed using the zip compression program. There are many types of compression programs used throughout the Internet. Luckily, the compression software is available to Internet users through FTP. To retrieve one of these compression programs for your own use, refer to the appendix on FTP (Appendix C) for an FTP address, directory locations, and file names for software archives which contain needed Internet and compression software. Once I downloaded the file "amd30.zip" and used my compression program to decompress the file, it was ready to install and run on my classroom computers.

As the students explored the new educational games, they were asked to assess their potential use and the skills that they would gain from such a program. The classroom scenario was such that the children could choose to purchase one program. Previewing each program enabled students not only to expand their knowledge of the current math concept, but also to explore consumer issues by assessing computer programs for their usefulness. The students did this by filling out a "Software Purchase Recommendation Form" (see Fig. 4–1). Many times throughout the school year, these recommendation forms were used to make actual purchases of computer software. When a purchase was not actually going to be made, students were told, but asked to fill out the recommendation form all the same.

As students become more familiar with software usefulness— not only as students, but also as consumers of computer software— this recommendation process can evolve into a classroom project. Each student is given a fictitious account, a checkbook, and a set amount of shareware bucks. The object is to purchase software that they feel will best suit specific needs. In one case, a group of students decided to look at primary education software. In previewing six programs written for first and second graders, this group of ten- and eleven-year-olds wrote a proposal to a first-grade teacher. In the proposal, the students explained the project, the software they previewed, and their recommendations. From this proposal, the first-grade teacher previewed the recommended shareware in his classroom and, with great approval from his students, purchased the program.

It was from this project that I realized the value and potential uses of FTP. This group of fifth graders empowered themselves to effectively change a first-grade classroom. They not only utilized the Internet and the FTP protocol, but also became commercial researchers and testers. The result of their work was formed into a pro-

---

Software Purchase Recommendation Form

Name: Date:

The title of the shareware software that I reviewed is:

This piece of shareware can be found on the Internet at the URL:

If the recommendation committee bought the program it would cost:

They would have to send the money to: (remember to look at the introduction of the program and in the pop down menus to find address information on the company or person that we would have to send money to)

This shareware program is: (describe the program in as much detail as you can)

It would be great for: (age, classroom, time in the day, etc.)

If you could buy five programs, would this one be one of your top five?

I recommend that this program be considered for purchase by the classroom.

I do not recommend that this program be considered for purchase by the classroom.

FIG. 4–1

fessional document that was useful and appreciated. How often do we as educators speak of empowering students to control their own learning, demystifying the educational process and bringing in real-world applications? The Internet, often called a slice of life, is in itself a link to the real world. A link that can be easily brought into the classroom.

A Picture Is Worth a Thousand Words

Every teacher knows how much a picture can enhance a lesson, help spark a child's interest, or bring a concept into focus. The Internet is filled with pictures and illustrations that can be very useful to any classroom, at any grade level. Perhaps a student is doing a research project on the anteater and is looking for a photograph for her research project; or you are looking for a photograph of Saturn to enhance an upcoming solar system lesson. You can guarantee that somewhere, someone on the Internet has the picture you are looking for. The question is, of course, where to find it. A good place to start is by looking in the graphics directory at "wuarchive.wustl.edu". Contained in this directory are hundreds of pictures and photos that may just match up with tomorrow's lesson plans.

Graphics and images on the Internet generally are in one of two different image formats, JPG or GIF. These images are easily viewed through one of many graphics programs. While many commercial programs will work on these graphics format types, there exist dozens of shareware graphics programs that can accommodate and view JPG and GIF graphics. To find such a program for you computer, turn to Appendix C and look under the shareware and freeware FTP sites listed.

For those of you who do not have a full Internet connection, FTP is bound to become an extremely valued tool. While there is no way to perform a subject search for FTP sites via FTP, it will take time to develop a list of FTP addresses that are helpful to you and your classroom. The appendix on FTP contained in this book is a start, but you should not hesitate to read the documents on FTP systems labeled mirrors, notes, or index. It is from these text-based documents that you are likely to find other anonymous FTP addresses suited to your needs. Checking out listservs and Usenet Newsgroups can also help you find new FTP resources. In Chapter 5 and Chapter 6, Gopherspace and The World Wide Web, we will be looking at other ways to discover useful FTP addresses, ways to search for FTP addresses, and ways to access them. While FTP may not become your classroom's number one use of the Internet, it can be a very helpful tool and is worth learning in order to maneuver among the remote systems.

FIVE

Gopherspace:
Finding Your Way

Revving up your 486 Pentium or your Power PC, you set your sights for the Information Super Highway. Dialing up your Internet service provider, you take the nearest on-ramp to the global network in search of the information and knowledge that you know is out there. Once on this super highway you are bombarded with unmarked off-ramps, construction signs, and blank signposts. In confusion, you pull off to the side of the road and search the contents of your glove box for an Internet map, only to find that, like the signpost, the map is blank.

The Internet of the seventies and eighties was not far removed from this imagined chaos of endless miles of highway, numerous off-ramps, and blank signposts. There were no maps to guide the journey, no gas stations to stop by and request help—only hundreds of vehicles searching for a place to go. At this time the Internet was being used by universities, governments, and large organizations with specific purposes in mind. They were not "surfing" the Net, but connecting to other libraries, colleges, and office contacts.

Gopherspace History

In 1991, this all changed, and the Internet began its journey into the mass media and the common household. At the University of Minnesota, a team of computer programmers were updating the campus' computer network. During this process, they created a menu-driven system that allowed students and faculty to access information on the network with ease and without archaic computer commands. This menu system developed into the Internet tool known as Gopher.

The concept behind the Gopher menu system was to create a computer menu that allowed users to find information, documents, and files with ease. This was done by creating a relationship between two computers on a network: client and server. The Gopher client is the user, while the Gopher server is the computer that is being accessed. As the client moves through the programmed Gopher menu, keystrokes are recorded and sent to the Gopher server. The server then accesses the appropriate information according to the keystroke commands and sends that information back to the client. The beauty of this relationship comes not in the ability to send and receive data (as this was already accomplished some twenty years earlier) but in the menu-driven system.

One year after the University of Minnesota announced their Gopher Menu system, the Internet had over 1,000 registered Gopher Menu sites. Today that number reaches well into the tens of thousands.

Gopher sites, like other Internet sites, are accessed via an Internet address—in this case, a Gopher address. Gopher addresses are very similar to those used by FTP and the World Wide Web, in that they consist of the domain name, which is a representation of the actual numeric address, and the computer name, separated by periods. When accessing a Gopher menu, the domain name is converted into the numeric address by your Internet service provider's domain server. From this numeric Internet Protocol (IP) address, your service connects you to the desired Gopher server. Once connected, the main Gopher menu is sent from the Gopher server to you, the Gopher client. The Gopher server then waits for keystroke commands which will in turn link you to other menus, documents, or files. Using the arrow keys or the mouse, you are able to maneuver through the Gopher menu to the next menu level. Through these virtual links you are able to control your journey through Cyberspace in an orderly, searchable manner.

Searching Gopher Space with Veronica and Jughead

While the development of Gopher menus made accessing and retrieving information from the Internet easy, the user was still faced with the dilemma of finding the needed information. On such a vast computer network like the Internet, this task was difficult and at times impossible. As Gopher menus became popular on the Internet, the evolution of Gopher search engines came into existence. Veronica and Jughead are two such Gopher search engines that allow users to search Gopher menus by keywords. The development of these search engines gave the Internet a new meaning and allowed common users to access information without prior knowledge of specific Gopher sites.

Veronica and Jughead can be accessed on many Gopher sites, one of the largest of which can be found at "gopher.ed.gov". You access this Gopher menu by either using a Web browser, such as Netscape for IP users, or through the UNIX command "gopher gopher.ed.gov" (see Chapter 6 for more information on using your Web browser to access Gopher menus). Once connected to the Gopher menu, a menu list is presented (see Fig. 5–1).

The third menu option is "Search This Gopher by Key Words (Jughead)." By moving to this menu option and pushing the right-hand arrow, you are presented with the search screen. At this point you can enter key words for Jughead to search. Typing the word "education," for example, produces a menu of 739 options, some of which are other Gopher sites dealing with education, while others are documents and files on the Department of Education's Gopher server.

Different Veronica and Jughead search engines will produce slightly different results (see Appendix D for Gopher addresses of interest to educators and students). When a key word search is entered into Veronica or Jughead, the Gopher site searches its data base on gopher menus for any Gopher site pertaining to your search. With each Veronica and Jughead Gopher site comes a different data base, hence a slightly different result in your search. In general the differences are minimal. Most searches will produce a similar result, starting with the larger Gopher menus. For example, the search via

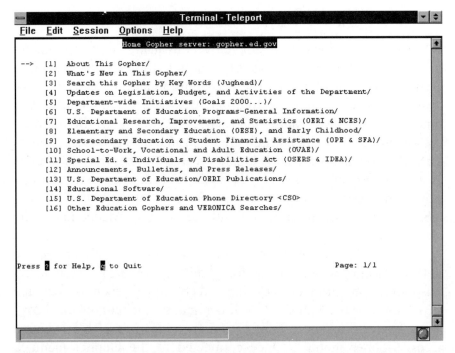

FIG. 5–1: *Main Gopher Page at gopher.ed.gov*

Jughead produced 739 sites and files. All of these sites and files are maintained on the Department of Education's Gopher server. A site search for the key word "education" done at the Veronica site "logic.uc.wlu.edu" will produce a list of 2,878 Gopher sites dealing with education. The major difference between these lists is that the Jughead search at the Department of Education's Gopher site searches for documents on its server only, while Veronica searched a data base of all known Gopher sites dealing with education.

Gopher for the Classroom: Teacher and Student Uses

Lesson Plans and Teaching Aids

Regardless of years of experience or filing cabinets filled with lesson plans and ideas, teachers are always on the lookout for new plans, new ideas, and new ways to teach the same concepts. Prior to the technology of the Internet, teachers had quenched this thirst by sharing ideas with others in their own buildings or seeking out colleagues at conferences or districtwide meetings, but these outlets provided only a handful of resources. The Internet allows us to share ideas with teachers from across the country and throughout the world. We have already explored this idea with email and newsgroups, which allow teachers to communicate with other teachers and to exchange information and thoughts. Gopher also allows teachers to find and gain new and refreshing ideas and lesson plans.

The BigSky Telegraph and the AskERIC archives are two places that can be found via Gopher menus and that contain a large number of creative and useful lesson plans. BigSky (bvsd.k12.co.us) is one of the more useful lesson-plan sites I have come across. Once connected to this Gopher site, you are presented with a menu of five choices. Each choice is a subject, such as math or science. It is within these menus that you will find some great ideas to enhance and enrich your curriculum.

The AskERIC archive is another fantastic place to find lesson plans, ideas, and teaching aids. Maintained at the Educational Resources Information Center (ERIC), a federally funded information center for educational resources, the ERIC archive provides educators with valuable professional information. At the same time, it allows teachers to submit their lesson plans to the archive, expanding their ability to share and communicate with other educators. To access the ERIC archive, go to their Gopher site "ericir.syr.edu". Once connected, you will be presented with a menu of educational resources. One choice among many is "Lesson Plans". It is within this menu choice that you will find the AskERIC lesson archive. Do not let your journey end there. ERIC offers teachers and others interested in education many resources for professional development and improvement.

After searching these two lesson-plan archives with the resources available to you through the Veronica and Jughead search engines, it is an easy task to search for other lesson plans on the Internet. By surfing to the gopher site at the University of Minnesota (k12.ucs.umass.edu) and entering the key words "lesson plans" into the Veronica search engine, I was able to obtain a list of over one hundred Gopher sites, all of which contain lesson plans for K–12 educators.

Student and Teacher Research

Gopher can bring into your school a world of information on nearly any subject desired. This technology lends itself easily to research and, with the Veronica and Jughead search utilities, even younger children can learn to use this resource.

The first step in searching Gopherspace is composing your key word search list. During an "I search" research project in my classroom, students composed research papers on different aspects of the world in the year 1492. Many of the students wished to use the resources available to them on the Internet. In doing so, their first task was to compose a list of words that they would use for their key word searches. In another situation, a second grader wished to find out more information about a specific type of dinosaur. With the help of an older student, this child entered the key word "dinosaur" into a Veronica search engine. The result was a Gopher menu with five options. Four pointed the child to Gophers that contained information on dinosaurs, and the fifth pointed to a Jughead search engine maintained at "dinosaur.umsl.edu". The first and fifth options were ruled out as good choices as the first was entitled "Barney the Purple Dinosaur" and the last was a search engine site that just happened to have the word "dinosaur" in its IP address. The other three choices included the "Dinosaur Unit (gopher.informns.k12.mn.us)", the "Dinosaur_National_Monument (ice.ucdavis.edu)", and the "Pointers to Dinosaur News (gate1.zedat.fu-berlin.de)" Gopher sites. From searching through these Gopher sites, this child not only gained some interesting knowledge about dinosaurs but also learned a lot about technology, word searches, and surfing Gopherspace.

From information on Africa at the University of Denver (omer-cury.cair.du.edu), to animals at the University of Pretoria (gopher.up.ac.za), to mountains at University Press Publications (aaup.pupress.princeton.edu) or oceans at the Ocean Information Center (gopher.cc.umanitoba.ca), Gopher menus can become a great resource of information in all aspects of the classroom. From teacher research to student research, Veronica and Jughead search engines can put a world-class library into any schoolroom across the country and throughout the world.

Parent Resources

School or classroom newsletters, parent nights, conferences, and daily communications with parents are all great ways to provide information to parents about learning, education, and special needs. Often, however, current information or the right information is not immediately available. With our private research stations—our computers connected to the Internet—information for parents and teachers about learning, education, and special needs is literally at our fingertips.

While connected to the Department of Education via Gopher at "gopher.ed.gov", I entered the key word "parents" into the Jughead search engine. As a result, I was presented with twenty-six articles and directories, all of which contain information about parents and education. From a new study about parents and young readers (dated only two weeks prior to my search) to a general information file for parents of various grade-level students to a document on how parents can help with school reform, the resources at this site are not only well written, but also pertinent and needed.

Approximately once a month, my students go home with the "Room 13 Update." This three- to four-page newsletter contains the normal classroom information, updates on the curriculum, content themes currently being studied, a calendar of upcoming classroom events, and a page that is dedicated to the Department of Education. Using abridged editions of the files from the Department of Education, I have printed and distributed various articles for parents to use as a resource. During the first portion of the year, the document "How Parents & Families Can Help Children Do Better in School" was sent out in the first classroom newsletter. Three days later a parent called wanting to know how she could get information similar to the article. As she has a Internet connection, I simply directed her to the Department of Education Gopher menu.

The same mother phoned again some six months later. At this time we were covering a curriculum unit on television usage, program content, violence, and sexism in cartoons and children's programming. She called to let me know that the Department of Education had a great article on "What Parents Need to Know About Children's Television Viewing." The article was included in the next Room 13 Update.

Another great resource not only for parents but also for teachers is the NOBLE Children's Library found on the North of Boston Library Exchange Gopher server (clsn1231.noble.mass.edu). From the main menu, follow the link to the NOBLE Children's Library where you will find library references and recommendations for children's books covering everything from arts and crafts ideas to science project books to story-hour recommendations. One of the most impressive menu choices available to you on this site is the link "Booklists for Children and Parents". Contained in this menu is a list of books that deal with issues that children often have to face, such as divorce, death of a loved one, a new baby in the house, or sleeping problems. This resource for children's literature has something for everyone and, for the literature-based classroom, may prove to be one of the most frequented places in Gopherspace.

Gopher did the one thing for the Internet that no other protocol could do: it organized it and made it accessible to the common user. Whether it be a new lesson on the solar system, a research project on the Holocaust, or information for parents and colleagues, Gopher menus can give you the information you are seeking. Veronica and Jughead will provide you with a detailed road map of the area, clearing a path for your journey and leading you directly to your destination. While Appendix D does list many Gopher addresses covering many subjects, do not hesitate to take the search engines out for a spin. It is by searching or surfing Gopherspace that you will find new and informative places on the Information Super Highway suited specifically to your needs.

SIX

The World Wide Web:
A Virtual Community

Email allows us to communicate with others, newsgroups give us a global electronic forum for communication, FTP puts software and documents of all kinds within our reach, and Gopherspace allows us to find, gather, and retrieve information with ease—but they all lack the graphical interaction that we have come to expect in today's age of multimedia. The World Wide Web (WWW) brought the Internet into the nineties with color, graphics, and user ease. The Web not only brought graphics from around the world to our computer screens, it also brought the national and international rush to get online. One year after the WWW was announced, the number of Internet users jumped from an estimated 3,913,843 to over 6,000,000 in six months. Today, there are approximately 45,776,375 Internet users and, according to Matrix Information and Directory Services (http://www.mids.org), this number doubles every year. By the year 2000 it is believed that an amazing three-quarter billion people, or nearly 13 percent of the world's population, will be online, and all of them will be connected to the World Wide Web.

May you be browsing through your local newspaper, watching TV, or reading your favorite magazine, you are bound to find an advertisement with a WWW address directing you to their WWW page. These advertisements are so numerous that it is hard to believe that the WWW came into existence only four years ago and that its popularity did not truly take off until 1994. Now in 1996, the term

"World Wide Web" has become synonymous with the Internet. In fact, many people believe that they are one and the same. However, the WWW is only a portion of the Internet. Like email, newsgroups, FTP, and Gopher, the WWW is an Internet protocol that allows information to be exchanged over a network of computers in a graphical, interactive method.

Two years ago I attended a conference on Telecommunications in the State of Oregon. During that conference, we met in small groups to confront the issues that arose in wiring the whole state for telecommunications. We also participated in a live teleconference with a panel in Virginia, worked with distant-learning technology, and experimented with many other forms of educational technologies. The most popular of these was a ninety-minute display of the WWW. Starting with the White House in Washington, we were guided through the U.S. Executive Branch, given a brief tour of the White House, and told some interesting facts about the Clinton household. I left this mini-session with a whole new vision of technology, of the Internet, and of its potential for education.

The Web Is Born: History in Brief

The history of the WWW takes us back to 1989 in Europe, where Tim Berners-Lee proposed to CERN (a collective of European high-energy physics researchers) a hyper-text project that would allow research members to transmit research papers and ideas in an organized and effective manner. The idea behind hypertext is that the reader can easily move from one area of the text to another. For example, throughout this book I have referred to figures, appendices, and other chapters. If you were reading this book on hypertext and you came across a reference to Appendix F, you would only have to select that reference to be instantly moved to the appropriate section of the book. Mr. Berners-Lee's proposal was recirculated in 1990 and the name World Wide Web was assigned to the project. At this time, the WWW was developed for the researchers at CERN and contained only text. The idea of video, sound, and graphics had not yet been considered.

Nineteen ninety-one proved to be a year of presentation for the WWW. From seminars in February, May, and June in the United States and throughout Europe, the idea of hypertext and the WWW became the hot topic in Internet technology. In August of the same year, hypertext files were made available on the Net through Usenet Newsgroups. This allowed the general Internet community the chance to read and discuss hypertext technology. In December, a major presentation and demonstration of the WWW was given at the Hypertext'91 Conference in San Antonio, Texas. This conference led to the release of the first publicly available Web browser in January, 1992, via anonymous FTP. This line-mode browser allowed the Internet community to access and view hypertext documents for the first time.

By January, 1993, fifty Hypertext Transfer Protocol (HTTP) servers were known, and .1 percent of the traffic on the Super Highway was being used for the WWW by March. Seven months later, two hundred HTTP servers were known and 1 percent of the traffic was accounted for by the Web. Later that same year, the WWW took off and entered into the common household through the famous "Internet in a box" kit sold by companies such as O'Reilly and Spry.

The Mosaic Web Browser was offered in these commercial packages and also became available via anonymous FTP throughout the Internet. Mosaic allowed the average Internet user to access HTTP documents with ease, incorporating text with graphics and spurring on the development of hundreds of Web sites. By late 1994 and early 1995, sound and video entered into the scene and the Netscape Web Browser was introduced.

Today, the WWW accounts for 30 percent of Internet traffic. It can be used to access hundreds of thousands of WWW sites and incorporates graphics, sound, video, and text into an on-line multimedia experience, an experience that can bring you into the virtual mountains of Tibet or the depths of the ocean to sift through the debris of the Titanic. It can provide you with information on the comet Shoemaker Levy or provide you with details on the latest movie produced by Disney.

Accessing the Web

Getting on the WWW is no different than reading your email, browsing through newsgroups, accessing FTP sites, or surfing Gopherspace. It does of course require an Internet connection and hypertext software, also known as a Web browser. Though the Mosiac Web Browser got us started with graphical interaction, Netscape has set today's standards. Previous beta versions of Netscape 1.0 are still available on the Internet; however, to gain the full appreciation of many Web pages, you will want to obtain a copy of the latest version of the Netscape Web Browser through a commercial software dealer. The WWW can also be accessed through a UNIX-based Internet account. However, through a dial-up UNIX account, the user will only see text. The general method used to access the Web through UNIX is with the command "lynx". This command will execute the Lynx line-mode Web browser—a text-based Web browser—and must be set up on your Internet service provider's network.

In order to surf the Web, either by way of a graphical Web browser such as Netscape or a line-mode browser similar to Lynx, you will utilize HTTP addresses and, like all other Internet protocol addresses, HTTP addresses indicate the desired location by way of an IP address. This address appears to us in words separated by periods. In most cases, HTTP addresses begin with "www", such as the Web pages for the Department of Education (www.ed.gov), and end with either "edu", "gov", "org", "net", "mil", or one of the many country codes discussed in the Introduction. When entering these addresses into Web browsers they are preceded with "http://". This indicates, not only to the Web browser but also to the Internet, that the address is to be used by the Hypertext Transfer Protocol (HTTP). The address in its entirety, "http://www.ed.gov", is called a Uniform Resource Locator (URL).

Directory information may also be a part of an HTTP address. This information is similar to directory information found on FTP. For example, the URL for the lesson-plan data base maintained at the AskERIC Web site (Educational Resources Information Center) is "http://ericir.syr.edu/Virtual/Lessons". The directory information

"/Virtual/Lessons" will point your Web browser directly to the lesson-plan data base. The HTTP address without the directory information, "http://ericir.syr.edu" will lead you to the main Web page of AskERIC. If you were to leave out the directory information, you would be able to get to your desired location through a simple hyperlink from the main page. However, this is not true for all Web pages, especially personal homepages that have been created by individuals on commercial service providers.

Personal homepages are created by Internet users throughout the world who wish to publicly announce their presence in Cyberspace. Many of these homepages provide you with some of the most valuable information, entertainment, and ideas found on the net. For example, my classroom's homepage can be found on my Internet service provider's network at the URL, "http://www.teleport.com/~kevcro". The directory information "/~kevcro" tells your Web browser to access the Web pages at "www.teleport.com" in the directory "~kevcro". Without this directory information, you would access the homepage for Teleport Inc., a large Internet service provider in the Northwestern United States. Though it is possible to find our homepage from Teleport's, it would be very difficult and time-consuming to do so, as Teleport has thousands of subscribers, each of whom may have a homepage stored on their network. With the directory information tagged onto the address, your Web browser will connect you directly to the desired homepage, in this case, directly to Room 13.

What the Web Has to Offer

The Internet and the WWW have been referred by many as a "cyber community," a form of "virtual reality." Cyberspace offers its community members information on everything, from entertainment to commerce, business, religion, and government. The Internet and the WWW can offer you and your students a slice of life. Literally name the subject, be it something educational such as the AIMS' Puzzle Corner page (http://204.161.33.100/Puzzle/PuzzleList.html) or something purely entertaining like the LEGO homepage (http://www.w-i-s.de/115001he.htm), the WWW is most likely to have what you are looking for. If you do not find it, then be assured that someone will be offering the information on the Web in the very near future.

In order to access the information of the WWW, you need to know where to go; you need the Internet address. Just like Gopher has Veronica and Jughead to aid in subject searches, the WWW also has its own set of search aids. These aids are called search engines and can search the WWW for reference to key words. One of my personal favorite search engines is Yahoo (http://www.yahoo.com). This search engine has maintained a presence on the Web for many years and thus has a very large data base of Web pages for you to search through. Once connected to the Yahoo page, you are presented with either a search option or a list of subject-oriented categories. From here, finding useful Web pages is only a few clicks away. For example, from the main page we can go to the category "Education". From there we are presented with a list of related subjects, one of which is "K-12". Clicking this link will produce a list of some twenty-one new categories which contain hundreds of hyperlinks. Most of these links will take us away from the Yahoo site and send us to a new WWW address. "Ensuring Equity and Excellence in Mathematics" is one such link found at Yahoo: Education: K-12: Educational Gender Equality (http://www.yahoo.com/Education/K_12/Educational_Gender_ Equity). This page is described as a resource for exploring gender equity in mathematics education. In selecting the link from the Yahoo page, you are moved to the homepage address of "http://www.ncrel.org/sdrs/areas/issues/content/cntareas/math/ma100. htm", the address for the "Ensuring Equity and Excellence in Mathematics" homepage. The address of the page that you are currently visiting is generally displayed near the top of your Web browser; this can vary depending on your specific browser.

Many times we are searching the Web for specific information. In this case the subject categories are not likely to be the most helpful. It is here that the use of key-word searches can be very handy. On the main page of Yahoo, you are given a box to type key-word searches into. A search done on the key words "Native American", for example, will give you a list of thirty-five Web pages, all of which provide you with Native American information in some form. This is obviously very useful in teacher and student research or even in simple Web-surfing fun.

While Yahoo tends to be my search engine of choice, there are many other search engines you may prefer. Each is set up slightly differently, some are more or less graphical, and some can even search multiple data bases at a time. Finding a preferred search engine on the Web is like finding a good friend. It must suit your needs, personality, and purpose. Turn to Appendix E for a list of many search engine addresses.

With Surfing the Web Comes Responsibility

As mentioned in the Introduction, administrators, teachers, and parents do not connect children to the Internet without first thinking of the risk. While it is important to note that children are not likely to come across questionable information without actively seeking it, the chance and the reality that they may access material and information not suited for them is a part of this virtual slice of life. If information not intended for children is going to be accessed, most likely it will be accessed via the WWW.

Search engines do not have age requirements, but they will search for key words such as "sex" or "erotic". These terms will produce a list of Web pages that are not intended for children. However, there are many ways to avert accessing these Web pages. Censorship by your Internet provider or by a software program such as CyberPatrol are two methods that can electronically block access to material. While these methods are popular they are not always 100 percent effective.

Web addresses close and open daily. A site may be operational one day, and shut down for no apparent reason the next. Censorship software relies on a data base of addresses that are not to be accessed. Some of the more recent software products offer monthly updates to keep the program's data base current. This not only creates a great commercial business, it also can give parents and teachers the idea that the system is secure for children. The fact is that with surfing the Web comes responsibility—the responsibility of adult supervision and the responsibility of the child. A computer connected to the Internet should be placed in a very visual area, not stuck in a back room or a closet of the library. Children as well as adults need to be educated and trained under the guidance of Appropriate Use Policies (AUP) as described in the introduction.

A Step Further—Empowering Students with a Web-Surfing Committee

Once policies are in place, rules are followed, and adult guidance is maintained, one can feel secure in allowing children to surf the Web. We, as teachers and parents, can take this security one step further by empowering children to be responsible for their own WWW choices. Many schools, classrooms, and homes have a list of favorite and approved Web sites that the children are free to visit. However, by the simple nature of hyperlinks, one page will link to another, which will link to another. This hyperlink function can inadvertently take you surfing on a wave in Cyberspace to an unknown destination. Pick any subject and find a Web page dealing with that subject. That page will most likely have a list of other Web pages, some dealing with the original subject, others not. Link to one of these sites, and in a few hyperlinks you are most likely going to find yourself at a Web page dealing with a totally different subject. Think of it like the game Telephone. With each link that takes you further from the original, the message is slightly changed. It is with this idea in mind that I recommend a list of classroom-approved sites along with a classroom approval committee made up of students. This committee maintains the approved list and accepts recommendations for new pages to be added to the list. This allows students to be accountable for their surfing time and information retrieval.

At the beginning of the school year, I present the children with a list of approved WWW sites. These are sites that I have visited in the past and that range from educational to entertaining. Basically, they have been placed on the Web to be used by teachers, families, and/or children. I gathered this list through a number of ways: my own personal surfing time, magazines on the Internet (i.e., NetGuide, which features a monthly section for kids online), district newsletters, news-groups aimed at teachers and children, and search engines and links from other homepages. Over the next few weeks, as the students and I work with the classroom AUP and the responsibilities of the Internet, we begin to explore search engines and links that are not on the class list. It is at this time that the "WWW Site Recommendation" form is introduced to the class (see Fig. 6–1). This form allows students to recommend a site they have visited to be placed on the class list permanently. From the recommendation form, students learn to document information they find on the Web as well as to gage the usefulness and appropriateness of the Web site. As recommendation forms are turned in, we review the recommended site as a whole class, looking into its content. This process takes about twenty minutes. If the class feels that the site is useful for education or entertainment and is appropriate, it is added to the classroom list of approved sites by category. As the class gains experience with the process, a committee is formed. The committee then meets as needed to review other recommendations.

This process may seem very time-consuming, but once the system is in place, it runs itself. It gives the children invaluable experience with the WWW and the Internet. They are given freedom to explore the Web on their own (with a teacher in the background) and they gain the power to directly influence their education. We have yet, as a classroom, to choose a site that has questionable material through this process, demonstrating the low risk of the process and the students' ability to discern between useful and nonuseful Web sites.

The Web and Beyond: Accessing FTP and Gopher Through Your Web Browser

As mentioned above, hypertext documents, or Web pages, are accessed through a line-mode Web browser, such as Lynx, or a graphical Web browser, such as Netscape. These browsers have the power not only to access hypertext documents through HTTP, but can also be used to access FTP and Gopher. To many users this is an advantage, as they do not have to learn to maneuver through three different

WWW Site Recommendation

I, _____, recommend that the World Wide Web site that can be found at URL, _____

_____

should be added to our classroom list of approved cites. The webmaster or owner of the site is _____, and they have put together a WWW site that can offer the class:

I have taken a look at most, if not all the sites linked to other sites. The linking pages are (in general)

It is my belief that this site should be added to the approved list because:

Sincerely,

FIG. 6–1: *WWW Site Recommendation Form*

software programs to access three different types of transfer protocols. The graphical Web browser also gives FTP and Gopher a more user-friendly appearance by employing graphics to represent the files and directory structures. They also allow use of the familiar point and click mouse function that we have all become accustomed to.

Accessing FTP and Gopher sites through Web browsers is very easy. If you recall, when accessing a World Wide Web site, you are using the Hypertext Transfer Protocol (HTTP). For that reason, all WWW addresses are preceded by "http://". This tells the Web browser what protocol to use. It works the same way for FTP and Gopher sites. For example, if we were to access the FTP site for the Sim-Tel Archives on a Web browser, we would need to enter "ftp://ftp.coast.net" as the requested address. That is the address for the requested site, "ftp.coast.net", preceded by "ftp://", which informs the Web browser to use the FTP protocol. When surfing to a Gopher site on a Web browser, the Gopher address is preceded by "gopher://", instructing the browser to use the Gopher transfer protocol.

It is also important to note that many Web browsers can also access email and newsgroups. However, this process is far from standard and varies greatly among different browsers. While it can make Internet use easier by being able to access all Internet-based information through one program, Web browsers were created and originally designed for HTTP. With the convenience of a single program may come the drawback of a slower connection, especially when using a slow modem connection to download large documents or programs.

Learning to Speak the Language of the Web: Writing HTML Code

The WWW brought the Internet much more than an organized, graphical way to retrieve information. It brought the power to reach out and give information back in the same organized, graphical manner. The WWW operates through a computer language known as Hypertext Markup Language (HTML). HTML is a very basic computer language, a language that any adult can learn and any child can learn with even greater ease. The code for HTML is made up of *tags* which are the commands that the Web browser reads. These tags are enclosed by the less-than and more-than symbols (<>). Anything outside of these symbols is treated as text and printed to the screen as is. The tags themselves are numerous, ranging from simple to complex. These tags, in conjunction with text information and graphics, come together to form the HTML document. This is simply a nonformatted text document, meaning that it is not written through a word processor, which saves formatting information (margins, font size, spacing, etc.) in the file; rather, the HTML document is saved as a plain text file, also known as ASCII.

Learning to speak the language of the Web is actually much easier than one would believe. The best way to begin your education is by taking a look at actual HTML code used on some of your favorite Web pages. You can do this by connecting to that Web site and then selecting the "source" command on your graphical Web browser. This is generally found in the "View" pull-down menu. Once you select this command, the Web browser will load and display the code that is used to create the Web page.

The first thing you will notice is that all HTML documents begin with the <HTML> tag and end with the </HTML> tag. The first tag states that all information to follow is coded in Hypertext Markup Language. The second closes the <HTML> tag. All HTML tags work in the same fashion, one tag executes a command, while the same tag is used with an added forward slash (/) to close or stop the command.

Let's take a look at a very basic HTML document. Figure 6–2 shows us what we would see if we were to view this document through a Web browser. Here is a copy of the HTML code that was used to code the Web page:

```
<HTML>
<TITLE>A Simple Web Page Example</TITLE>
<BODY>
<CENTER>Welcome to our Web Page</CENTER><P>
<CENTER>Enjoy your visit!</CENTER>
</BODY>
</HTML>
```

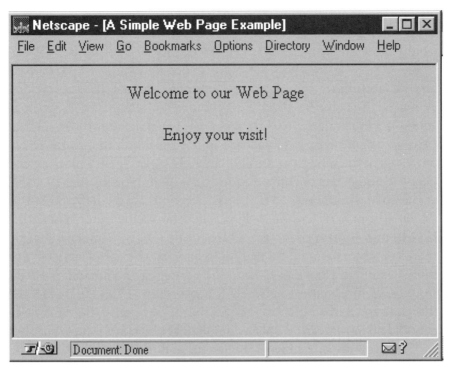

FIG. 6–2:   *A Simple Web Page Example*

Notice the document begins with <HTML> and ends with </HTML>. Next comes the title tag. This tag tells the Web browser what the title of the page is. The browser uses this information to place the title of the page in the top bar of the browser screen. As you can see in the HTML code, the title is typed between the opening <TITLE> tag and the closing </TITLE> tag.

The body tag can vary greatly from one Web page to another. While it will always be present, different functions may be included inside the opening <BODY> tag. This tag signifies the body of the code, like the body of a report. If the code is opened with <BODY> only, the page will be displayed like the one in Figure 6–2. However, if you wish to get a little creative with your Web pages, you can change the background and text color from within the <BODY> tag. This is done by using "BGCOLOR" and "TEXT" commands. For example, to display the same Web page as in Figure 6–2 but with background color changed to blue and the text color changed to red, the body tag would now appear as <BODY BGCOLOR="00CCFF" TEXT= "990000">. The numbers are color codes known as RGB, or Red, Green, and Blue. These codes represent colors; as the code is changed, the color for the background will change as well. You can access a color chart of RGB codes at Doug Jacobson's homepage (http://www.phoenix.net/~jacobson/rgb.html). All other tags are left unchanged, including the closing body tag, </BODY> which appears near the end of the document, telling the Web browser that the body of the code is complete.

Finally, in between the body tags lies the Web page. It is here that HTML tags control the look and feel of the Web document. Images, sounds, and text can all be manipulated with the use of various tags. In our example I have used only the center tag command. This tag centers all information between the opening <CENTER> tag and the closing </CENTER> tag. Other basic tags can be found in Appendix F. By no means is this a complete list of HTML tags, but they will help you get started with the language of the Web.

Learning as you go is the key to learning any language, even a computer language. Write a little code, save it, and check it with your Web browser. If it did not look as you anticipated, try to find the problem. Looking at other pages on the Net will also give aid to learning the uses of various tags. If you come across a Web page on the Internet that has a look you like and that has a graphic specifically placed to the left or right of the page or a combination of large- and small-sized text, take a look at the source code through your browser. See what tags were used and how they were used. Then try the code with your own document.

You can also seek help learning HTML code by picking up one of the many books available at your local bookstore or by turning to the Web itself. The Web not only can provide you with excellent examples of HTML code through the source command on your Web browser, but also has many helpful Web pages dedicated to teaching and learning HTML. You can find some useful Web pages that provide information on HTML code in Appendix E or turn your Web browser to Yahoo's Computers and Internet, World Wide Web, HTML, Guides and Tutorials page at "http://www.yahoo. com/Computers_and_Internet/Software/Data_Formats/HTML/ Guides_and_Tutorials/". There you will find eighty-eight Web pages listed, all of which are dedicated to helping you learn to speak the language of the Web.

Bringing Your Knowledge into the Classroom: Teaching Children to Speak HTML

Once you begin to master the fundamentals of HTML coding, you may wish to bring the concept into the classroom. Coding HTML is an excellent way to work on problem-solving skills and sequencing. In order to introduce a classroom of children to the coding process, I designed a project that would incorporate many aspects of the classroom routine. We started our coding project by working through the writing process. As a whole class, we explored the idea of a metaphor. As the concept became clearer, we read through a number of metaphor poems found in various children's poetry books. The classroom then created a collaborative metaphor poem. A picture was added to the poem by a number of students, and one illustration was voted on. As the students turned to independent work in creating their own metaphors, I prepared a lesson that would aid the students in developing a Web page for their poetry. The students began to complete their poetry and art work and we turned back to a whole group setting and began to look at basic HTML command tags.

Over the course of a few days, students worked with very basic examples of HTML. Using a list of tags, students were presented with a printed sample Web page and in small groups wrote a HTML document that would produce the same effect. This practice led us to work with the collaborative metaphor poem. By following the guide in Figure 6–3, we worked as a whole group coding the classroom poem and discussing the tags. Over the next couple weeks, students worked in groups of two during class time, coding their poems with the aid of the "Coding Your Metaphor Poem" guide.

The students had some previous experience with the computer,

Coding Your Metaphor Poem

- Above your poem you will need the html tag and the body tag.
    - `<HTML>`
    - `<BODY BGCOLOR="#ffffff">`

- Below your poem you will need the closing body and html tags.
    - `</BODY>`
    - `</HTML>`

- In between the top `<HTML>` tag and the `<BODY>` tag you want a title tag. This tag will give your web page a title at the top of the screen.
    - `<TITLE>Type your title here</TITLE>`

- Now, take another look at the top `<BODY>` tag. Notice the part that reads
    - `BGCOLOR=`
    The numbers that follow the equal sign name the color of the screen background. If you would like to change the color, which is set at white, then use the RGB color chart and change the RGB number.

- Center the title of your poem by using the `<CENTER>` tag. Be sure to turn that tag off at the end of your poem, before the `</BODY>` tag with `</CENTER>`.

- Between your poem title and your poem, you will want to put a paragraph break, `<P>`. And at the end of each line of your poem, you will want to put a line break, `<BR>`. This will make sure that your poem prints on the screen in separate lines, not just one big long line.

- At the bottom right before the `</CENTER>` and `</BODY>` tags, type the following to put a link at the bottom of your page back to the classroom page:

    `<P><IMG SRC="line10.gif"><P>`
    Return to the `<A HREF="metaphor_poems.htm">Poem Index</A>` page.

- Finally, you need to add your picture to your HTML code. Right after the `<CENTER>` tag, type:

    `<IMG SRC="name.gif"><BR>`

    (Type your name instead of the word "name".) This will tell the web browser to load your graphic right before it prints your poem.

FIG. 6–3

word processors, and scanners, and this experience became the foundation from which we could learn and experiment with the HTML code. Those who took to the code easily became the classroom experts and were called upon by other students as problems were encountered. In its entirety, the project took over three weeks and the result was incredible. Each student had created a Web document, choosing the graphics and the colors in creating his or her own slice of our classroom's homepage.

The metaphor poem pages were linked to our homepage and we invited people in Cyberspace to come and visit. Through Usenet Newsgroups and a couple classroom/student-oriented listservs, we wrote a brief description of our project, asking people to stop by and give us feedback. The most incredible feedback we received was from the East Coast. A woman had read our poems and enjoyed them very much. She emailed the classroom, complimenting the students on the work, and asked two students in particular if she could read their poems to her daughter's classroom. The students eagerly agreed. One week later, we received email from her again. She wanted Lauren, the author of the poem in Figure 6–4, to know that an artist friend of hers wanted to draw illustrations for each line of her poem. Lauren agreed and anxiously awaits the results of the artist's work.

From one writing project, students gained experience in many areas of education. Working through the writing process, they expanded their creativity and writing skills, developing poems and illustrations. The WWW served as an outlet to examine and experiment with multimedia presentations and allowed students to display their work to the world. And the world responded, demonstrating to these children in a concrete fashion that their creative work is appreciated, valued, and enjoyed by others from Oregon to New Jersey and beyond.

World Wide Web Projects and Surfing Ideas

The World Wide Web offers the classroom a worldwide connection in a way that no other part of the Net can. It allows us to experience education in a room without walls, without limits. It gives us

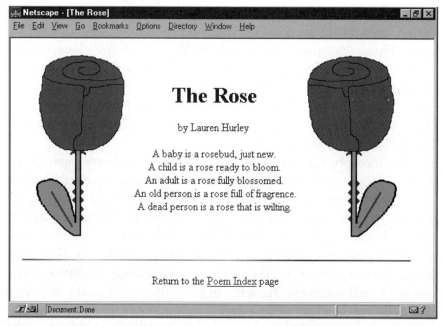

FIG. 6–4: *Lauren's Poem*

the potential to share our classroom with anyone who wishes to stop by for a visit—and they do not even have to check in at the office. It allows us to make connections with people from around the world, bringing their cultures and histories into our schoolhouse. It gives us a graphical medium by which we can reach out to billions of others—students, teachers, and world citizens. It not only gives us a global community that we can relate to and experience, but also offers a community that we can join.

In Chapter 7 we will be taking a closer look at the WWW in the classroom by looking at a year on the Net in a fifth-grade room. Many of the WWW projects found throughout that chapter require the use of a classroom homepage. The projects listed below, however, are intended to focus on Web surfing. It is estimated that there are some eighteen million Web pages in Cyperspace and this number doubles every fifty-six days. A large majority of these pages are perfect for teacher and student research and classroom projects; some, in fact, are specifically designed for it.

Research

Long-term research projects can often be difficult in a classroom. While they are essential for the development of investigative, problem-solving, and independent-thinking skills, classrooms are often faced with limited research resources. The Internet and the WWW can put volumes of research knowledge in your classroom or in your school. By simply turning your Web browser to one of the many search engines (see Appendix E) such as Yahoo (http://www.yahoo.com), or the Web-crawler (http://www.Webcrawler.com/), you and your students can begin to search for information by key words.

I have found it helpful for both the children and myself first to have students make a list of key words that will aid in narrowing their search. This gives them time to think about their search off-line, thus spending less time on the very popular and very busy computer.

After students enter their key-word search, they are presented with a list of Web pages or links that will provide them with information on their topic in some form or another. From here students learn to sift through information, deciding what is useful and accurate. We do this with direct instruction. During the first portion of the year, when the children are just being introduced to the Internet and the idea of using it as a research tool, we take a look at the information we can find. Web pages often tell you where their information is from—this will give us a good idea if the information is trustworthy. We also look at the site address. When doing research, my class prefers to rely on sites that end in "edu" for we know that this domain name is given only to educational facilities.

Research on the Web gives students incredible experiences with today's technology, preparing them for the future. They become experienced with information retrieval and telecommunications while at the same time learn to judge information for its value and creditability.

The Library of Reviews

As a student and as a teacher, I have never enjoyed book reports. As a student, I hated having to do them; as a teacher, I hate having to assign them. It is for that reason that I created the Library of Reviews for the classroom. At first the Library of Reviews was a five-by-seven-inch card file box where students would submit a review of a book for others in the classroom to read. These reviews are treated as professional reviews, not unlike those you would find in journals or magazines. Students are to tell others their impressions of the book and their recommendations.

As Room 13 developed its own homepage, it occurred to me that the Library of Reviews could easily be put on the Net for others to use. The on-line library is still very much in its infancy with under a hundred reviews listed in the author and theme indexes. However, it does allow children ages fifteen and under to read reviews of books written by their peers. It also allows children to submit their own reviews to be archived and listed in the indexes.

The response to the Library of Reviews has been fantastic. In its first three months of production, we received many reviews from throughout the United States as well as from our own classroom. One young boy emailed us with a review of a famous R.L. Stine book. In the review he thanked us for telling him about the Goosebumps book series. He said, "though they may not be my father's favorite choices, they are mine. I never really read before your page introduced me to these books. I love em'." While I readily agree with his father's opinion, the latter point says it all. The Library of Reviews is about children, children reading for enjoyment and sharing with others their age.

The Library is located among the Room 13 Web pages and can be found at URL, "http://www.teleport.com/~kevcro". Once there, follow the link to the "Library of Reviews".

Sharing Your Work with the World

Whether or not your classroom has developed a personal homepage, you can still share your work with the world. In previous chapters we discussed this idea by way of email, listservs, or Usenet Newsgroups. The Web also offers your classroom and your students this ability.

The Library of Reviews is one such method where students can share their thoughts and work with the world. The Peace in Pictures Project is another. The Peace in Pictures Project, located in Jerusalem, Israel, is a Web page dedicated to pictorial representations of peace done by children of all ages from all around the world. The page invites children to send in pictures they have drawn that represent what peace means to them and what peace looks like to them. Children submit their pictures by either mailing, emailing, faxing, or uploading the pictures to the Peace in Pictures Project FTP site. From there the picture or photograph is scanned and added to the projects Web page.

To share in this project, surf to "http://www.macom.co.il/peace" and take a journey into a child's peaceful world. When you are there, do not forget to write down the projects mailing information. Get out a box of crayons and start drawing your vision of peace for all the world to see.

Welcome to Our Classroom

As schools get connected to the Internet, the ability to develop classroom Web pages becomes available, and schools and classroom are taking advantage. With every classroom, regardless of the level, comes a different group of children, a different group of teachers, and a dynamic of personalities, thoughts, ideas, and projects that are truly unique. The Web gives each of our schools and classrooms the chance to share their uniqueness and to learn about others, like ourselves, in a way that has never before been possible.

Finding schools and classrooms online has become as easy as finding the White House online, through WWW search engines. Yahoo maintains a page of hundreds of schools and classrooms at "http: //www.yahoo.com/Education/K_12/". "The HotList of K-12 Internet School Sites" (http://www.sendit.nodak.edu/k12) and the "Web66 International Registry of School Web Sites" (http://Web66.coled. umn.edu/schools.html) are search sites that are dedicated to schools and classrooms. At these sites you will find links to schools and classrooms throughout the United States and the world, often categorized by state and country to make your search that much easier.

Virtual Museums

In today's national funding crisis, it is becoming more and more difficult to continue classroom field trips and off-campus projects. While we as teachers will never be able to replace trips that bring our children out into the world to experience its wonders, we can supplement the trips that we do have with virtual museums on the WWW. In fact, some virtual museums can take us places that would never be possible, regardless of our field-trip budget.

Virtual museums can be found throughout the Web and come to us from every corner of the world. Ranging from actual museums like the Smithsonian in Washington and the Louvre in Paris to museums found only on the Net, such as the "1492: An Ongoing Voyage" Web site, these museums bring tours, pictures, sounds, information, and experiences into our classroom that no other resource can.

In the Introduction of this book, I played on a scenario that started with a virtual tour of the Louvre (http://mistral.culture.fr/louvre/) and ended with children producing their own art work using the artistic elements of great historical painters. The Louvre Web site offers educators the ability to view hundreds of famous paintings that hang on the museum's walls and throughout the world. Another link from the Louvre will take us on a graphical tour of Paris, complete with history, architecture, and tourist information. The museum's Web site provides classrooms outside Paris with the closest thing to reality, with more information on the art world, the artists, and Paris than we would be able to consume, even if the Concorde become our school bus.

For aquatic animal fans, there is the Sea World Web site. Not only is this a great site to wander through and to view and learn about the different animals found at Sea World; it also serves as a fantastic research site for animal reports. The site contains many pictures of various animals and an animal data base with information on many aquatic animals. Teachers can get information on Sea World's educational material and programs, as well as ideas to aid in lesson planning and enrichment.

Another favorite Web site of mine is "1492: An Ongoing Voyage" (http://sunsite.unc.edu/expo/1492.exhibit/Intro.html). An exhibit of the Library of Congress in Washington, this site offers a guided tour through the world of 1492, dealing with tough issues of European contact with the Americas. Divided into six sections, this page will take you and your students on a voyage of discovery from "What came to be called America" before European contact, to "Christopher Columbus: Man and Myth". Though this site does not offer the rich graphics that other museum pages do, it is rich with textual information and a spatter of original maps and drawings from 1492. It is a must-see resource for teachers and students studying the "discovery" or the "rediscovery" of the Americas.

Museums online are coming alive each day, bringing to the class-room a rich source of information and experiences that simply are not possible due to geographic location or budget restraints. Search engines are a great place to get started searching for your favorite museums throughout the world. Appendix E contains a list of some search engine sites that can help as well as a list of many museums and virtual tours that Room 13 has found inviting.

Teaching and Parenting Resources on the Web

Throughout the Internet, there exist resources for every profession and every person online, including teachers and parents. One of the underlying purposes of this book is to point out those resources to you. Teachers and parents are two groups of people in our communi-ties who always seem to be on the search for information, ideas, and thoughts on how to better ourselves, our tasks, our children.

For teachers, the Web allows us to gather ideas and enrich lesson plans. Through Web pages like the ones found on the U.S. Depart-ment of Education's Web site (http://www.ed.gov), the AskERIC Web site (http://ericir.syr.edu), and the Library of Congress (http://www.loc.gov), we are able to access information about our profession, lesson plans, available financial grants, and opportunities provided to us by private and governmental agencies through the United States.

Individual Internet users have also dedicated their time to en-hancing our resource availability by collecting and maintaining links to sites of interest to teachers, parents, and students. The Busy Teach-ers' WebSite (http://www.ceismc.gatech.edu/BusyT) is one personal homepage created by Carolyn Cole, a former teacher whose goal it is to supply teachers, parents, and lifelong learners with resource links that will help to relieve their work load and quench their desire for knowledge. This site is the home of hundreds of WWW links to educational Web sites, lesson plans, activity ideas, and resource materials found around the world. The sites are separated into categories from archaeology to social studies and even include a teacher's reference section for searching ease. It is not only a jewel of a resource but also a tribute to our profession.

Parents and teachers will also find the links and information at the National Parent Information Network (NPIN) (http://ericps.ed. uiuc.edu/npin/npinhome.html) very interesting and useful. The NPIN's purpose is to provide valuable parenting information. This Web site contains resources and links to various parenting materials and information that can be found in the AskERIC archives and throughout the Web. Other pages created by individual Internet users, like Uncle Bob's Kids Page, provide current parenting information and important Web-linked resources.

For a more complete list of parent resources, turn to Yahoo's parenting resource page at URL, "http://www.yahoo.com/Society_and_ Culture/Families/Parenting" as well as Appendix E.

Surfing Fun: Safe, Entertaining Fun on the Net

I will end this chapter on the note of surfing fun. There are great resources available to us through the WWW. Many of these exist purely for our entertainment and surfing enjoyment. These sites bring out the playfulness of the human spirit and entice our curiosity to really go surfing in search of the fascinating, interesting, funny Web site. However, setting a child loose on the Web to surf carries with it the dangers previously mentioned. In response to creating a safe place in Cyberspace for our younger community members, many people have created child-safe Web sites filled with hyperlinks to entertaining Web sites of all kinds.

Uncle Bob's Kids Page (http://gagme.wwa.com/~boba/kids.html) is one good place to get you started. This site has well over a hundred links to other pages that are designed with children in mind, like the CyberKids Launchpad (http://www.woodwind.com/mtlake/CyberKids/ Launchpad.html) and the Michael Jordan Page (http://miso.wwa.

com/~boba/mj.html). Uncle Bob has even included sections on safe surfing and parent resources.

Yahoo has a section designed especially for children at the URL, "http://www.yahoo.com/Society_and_Culture/Children/Links_for_ Kids", as do many other search engines on the Web. One site that is always a hit on the Yahoo Links for Kids page is the "Safe for Kids Site of the Week." Each week this site chooses a new Web page to highlight. The weekly choice has been reviewed and determined safe and enjoyable for kids. There choices range from interesting museum tours to sites on slimy creatures, snakes, and reptiles. Yahoo also offers a Web guide for kids entitled, "Yahooligans!" which can be found at "http://www.yahooligans.com".

The World Wide Web can bring the wealth of the world into our classrooms. From a research tool to a play toy, the WWW provides adults and children with information, graphics, sounds, and multimedia from all corners of the world. It can be used to enrich our ideas and lesson plans, expand our thinking and experiences, and tear down the walls of the classroom that keep us limited in our educational careers. The WWW simply brings us together in a virtual global community, allowing us to share our lives and our work with others regardless of geographic barriers.

SEVEN

Creating a Classroom Presence on the Web: A Year in Brief

Where There Is a Will . . .

In November, 1994, I returned to my classroom of fourth graders from a telecommunications conference held by the state of Oregon. I walked into the classroom refreshed and excited about the Internet and its potential for classroom use. I opened the door, and my excitement and plans were slammed back into reality. Faced with the four walls, twenty-nine desks, and two Apple IIe computers, I realized that everything I wanted to do with the Internet, all I wanted to bring into the classroom for students' use and experience, was not possible.

Meanwhile, as the classroom continued its previous course, I began to experiment with the Net at home, learning email, newsgroups, Gopher, and the WWW through the Lynx text-based Web browser. I was overwhelmed with the tools the Internet could bring and frustrated with my inability to bring these tools into the classroom. In January, 1995, I received a donation of a 286 IBM compatible computer, and for the first time had the compatibility between my computer at home and a computer at school. I could now bring files from home and access them from my classroom.

This reminded me of a concept I had heard about where teachers use their home computer, connected to the Internet, as a way to access Internet resources from the classroom. Saving files from the Internet to disk, I could bring email and newsgroups into the classroom where students could begin to experiment with these tools. Termed the "Sneaker Net," as the networked data is be carried from one computer to the next by foot, my students began to learn about the Internet in a very basic fashion. As a whole class, we had many discussions about the function of the Internet, what type of information and resources it can offer, and the basics of how the global network was started. In the process of these discussions, the idea of keypals was brought up. We composed a Usenet Newsgroup letter and generated a list of applicable newsgroups to post the letter to. Over the next week, I brought in responses to our request for a classroom keypal group as well as newsgroup posts from other teachers who had also written letters about classroom keypals. By Friday, we were all set with a classroom in Virginia and the first group of letters was drafted.

Using the writing process, students drafted their letters, edited them cooperatively, then published them by typing them into the 286 computer. By Tuesday all the students had typed their letters into the word processors, the file was saved to disk, and I brought it home with me that evening. Once at home, I opened the file, copied the letters via the copy function, and pasted them into the email letter. We were off and running—our first formal email had been sent and the class began their journey into Cyberspace.

The remainder of the year continued like this. I used my home connection to upload and download email and newsgroup posts and writing to our keypal classroom. Thus, we experienced the Internet through the Sneaker Net method. A few students became very interested in the international connection that the Internet had to offer and posted letters to the "alt.elementary.chat" newsgroup seeking keypals from foreign countries. Soon, not only were we writing to the classroom in Virginia, but individual students were writing to keypals in Germany, Australia, Singapore, and Japan.

By the end of the school year, we were working with three donated IBM compatible computers, all 286s, all in working order. We had also acquired a 486, a highly capable computer, that was to be shared with many other classrooms. My excitement returned as I realized that this new computer could provide us with a means to experience the Web side of the Internet by designing, planning, and writing Web documents in the classroom, then uploading them to my Internet server at home.

However, it was the end of the year and time was running out. Designing Web pages would not be possible this year, but we were leaving the classroom for the summer with the knowledge that the following year we would all be together again, this time as a fifth-grade classroom. We ended our introduction to email and newsgroups with final letters to our keypals and, in many cases, the exchange of snail mail (land mail) addresses. The computers were turned off, the classroom cleaned up, and the doors locked with the hope that next year, Room 13 could truly become a part of the electronic global community.

Developing an Integrated Internet Experience

Right before the end of the school year, a parent came to me with a copy of *EARTHSEARCH: A Kids' Geography Museum in a Book*. On page 103 was a story about a primary classroom in Australia who had "launched GeoBears." The idea was that each child gave a stuffed animal to a friend who was traveling out of the area. The bear was equipped with a name tag and an explanation of the project, complete with the address of the classroom. Once the friend reached her destination, the bear was passed to someone else, each time the bear's traveling companion would collect souvenirs and send home letters about the bear's journey.

Through the summer months this idea stayed with me. By midsummer I had formulated the basis of our fifth-grade geography program by using and adapting the GeoBear concept. I had begun to experiment more fully with HTML coding, and the idea of integrating a classroom Web page around the GeoBear project struck me as feasible.

My desire was to fully integrate Internet technology into the classroom. With the GeoBear project as a vehicle, I came up with a Web-page design that would integrate writing, social studies, and geography. The first step in putting together our Web page was to map out the information that we would want to display on the Net. In thinking about our GeoBear project, I developed a mind map that became our classroom Web page (see Fig. 7–1). This page contained introductory information about the Geo and Terra project, along

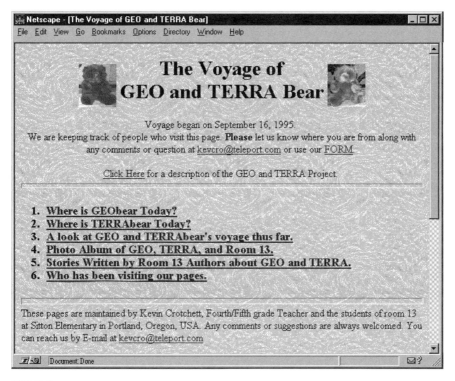

FIG. 7–1

with hyperlinks to other pages for the classroom to use and develop, such as the Where is GeoBear Today? page.

As the new school year began, backpacks where sewn onto the bears' backs and a photo album was filled with pictures of the classroom preparing for Geo and Terra's departure. For two weeks we played with the bears, talked about and prepared for the voyage, and wrote stories during writers workshop time using the bears as central characters. Geo and Terra's departure date quickly approached. It was time to begin advertising our upcoming project and our classroom Web pages on the Internet. By turning to newsgroups, listservs, and WWW search engines, we let the Cyberspace community know about our project and invited them to visit our Web pages. Photos were scanned and added to their own space on the Web as were stories written by the students (see Figs. 7–2, 7–3). These pages were

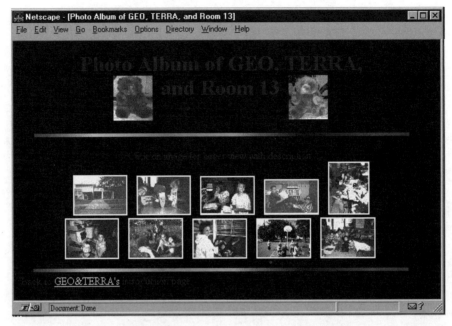

FIG. 7–2

then linked to the main homepage of The Voyage of Geo and Terra, and our Internet project was under way.

On September 16, 1996, in the company of two students selected by lottery, Geo and Terra left Portland, Oregon, by way of the Portland International Airport in the care of two newly found friends. They were bound for San Diego, California, and St. Louis, Missouri, respectively. The following Monday, with departure information in hand, we updated the Web pages and marked the information on a classroom wall map of Geo and Terra's journeys. A few days later we received our first email messages from Utah. A classroom had visited our Web pages and wanted to let us know they had stopped by. A map pin was place on Utah, marking our guest's location in the world, and their email message was added to Geo and Terra's Travel Log.

Over the next few months we continued to hear word of Geo and Terra's journeys by snail mail and email, as well as receiving email letters from people who were visiting our pages. As letters arrived, maps

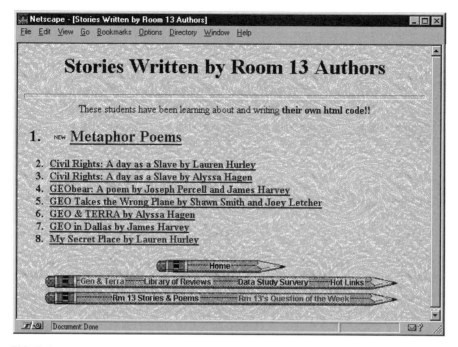

FIG. 7–3

and Web pages were updated and new stories were created. By November, we had unfortunately lost contact with Geo, but were reassured by Terra's incredible journey in St. Paul. It was at this time that we began the Geo and Terra update. This was a Room 13 student production newsletter which contained information on Geo and Terra's journeys complete with maps and interviews. Stories from classroom authors were added along with pictures when available. This newsletter was then mailed by land to those people who had thus far been involved with our project and to neighboring schools and administrative officials, furthering the advertising process of our Web presence.

Expanding Our Presence on the Web

By January, 1996, the Voyage of Geo and Terra was slowing down. We had not heard from Geo in nearly three months. Terra was on her way to Florida after a beautiful trip in Hawaii. We had just received a package from Terra, with pictures and souvenirs from her Hawaiian voyage, but email to the Web pages was dwindling as was the excitement for the project. It was time to add to the classroom presence on the Web and to rekindle the children's energy with this technology.

The Library of Reviews and the Room 13's Question of the Week Listserv was introduced. The Library of Reviews is a data base of book reviews of children's books, written by children (see Fig. 7–4). This gave Room 13 a medium for other children on the Web to interact with. The concept is that children can submit a review to the library. That review is then categorized by the classroom and linked to our Web pages.

The Room 13's Question of the Week came from a student in the classroom who had seen a commercial for AT&T. The commercial was about children answering questions on the Internet and sharing those answers with others. After discussing the format that the class would like to see the project take, I went back to my computer and learned about the Internet technology of listservs. With help from my Internet service provider, the listserv "rm13-l@teleport.com" was developed and the Question of the Week listserv was online. Students then advertised the listserv, asking classrooms and individuals to join. Two weeks later the first question was posted, "Would you rather swim like a fish or fly like a bird?" Our responses to the question were posted to the listserv as other members posted theirs.

By the end of school year we had twenty-six listserv members from four countries—the United States, Canada, Germany, and Israel—responding to our questions and sending in their own suggestions for the following week. The responses were saved and archived each week on the Room 13 homepage as advertisement of the listserv and growth in membership continued.

With the addition of these two classroom Web projects came the dilemma that our main Web page, the Voyage of Geo and Terra, could no longer adequately represent our classroom on the Internet. We needed to develop a more general introductory page that would guide our guests to the project that they wished to visit. With some investigation into my school building's telephone service, I found an

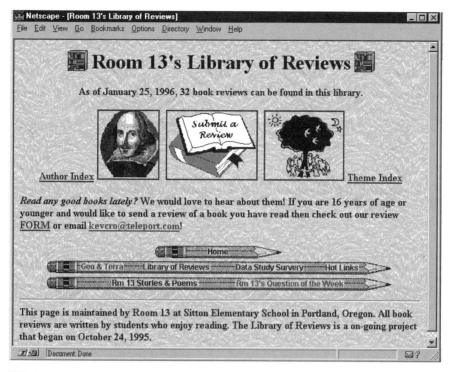

FIG. 7–4

unused phone line in a back room. From this phone line I was able to introduce students to the on-line Web experience a few at time. During these surfing voyages, we discussed page layout and began to develop a working concept for HTML coding. Back in the classroom, a Room 13 Web page was created, one that would represent all our links equally (see Fig. 7–5).

Surveying the Cyberspace Community: A Lesson in Data Study

Room 13's last major Web project was in the form of a data study. During a unit on statistics, we began to survey the school for the famous loose ear lobes and ability to twist one's tongue. This brought one of the students to develop a survey questionnaire during a free exploration writers' workshop time. This letter was then posted to a number

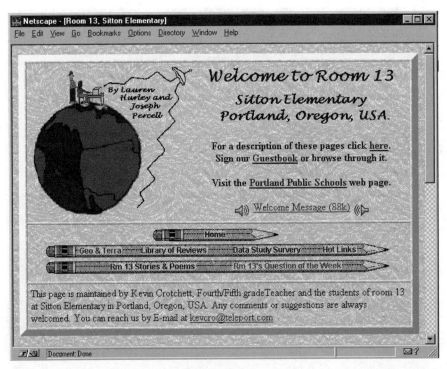

FIG. 7–5: *Welcome to Room 13 Homepage*

of newsgroups asking people to respond via email. As responses came in we began to discuss the possibility that our data from this printed survey may not be correct because the people reading the survey had no pictures of loose lobes or twisting tongues. In response, the data study Web page was linked to Room 13 (see Fig. 7–6).

This page presented a survey on loose lobes and twisting tongues and allowed guests to fill out the survey and email their results to the classroom. The page was advertised once during the final two weeks of school. We received over fifty-six surveys from children and adults in the United States, Canada, England, and France. Their surveys were added to our study and the statistics were calculated.

The World Wide Web and the Internet focused our classroom on long-term integrated projects that incorporated the world as our audience and our classmates. It allowed us not only to display our work

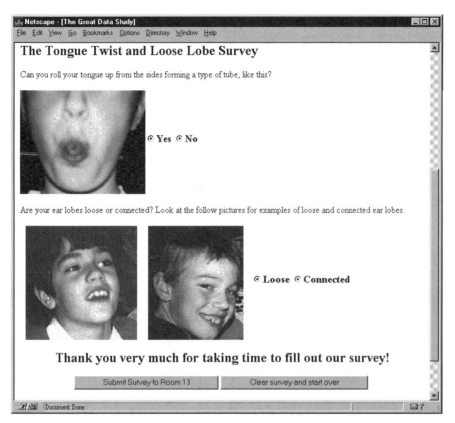

FIG. 7–6

in a global hallway, but also to invite a global community to partici-pate in our learning process. It broke down classroom walls, introduc-ing us to new friends throughout the world. In nine months, we communicated with hundreds of people of all ages, from seven coun-tries and many cultures. The Internet brought us a technology for learning, communicating, and interacting with the human race—a technology that needs to be marveled rather than feared. Email key-pals started our journey through Cyberspace. Like outer space, which continues to expand into the cosmos, the Internet grows and expands daily, allowing our voyage to continue as we travel the roads of the Information Super Highway.

Listservs of Interest to Teachers and Students

Art

International Society for Education Through Art (INSEA-L)
    INSEA-L@UNBVM1.CSD.UNB.CA (list)
    LISTSERV@UNBVM1.CSD.UNB.CA (listserv)

NMAA Art Curriculum Teacher Conference TEACHART
    TEACHART@SIVM.SI.EDU (list)
    LISTSERV@SIVM.SI.EDU (listserv)

Curriculum

AERA-B Division B: Curriculum Studies Forum (AERA-B)
Intended to promote the exchange of information among scholars and researchers engaged in curriculum studies.
    AERA-B@ASUVM.INRE.ASU.EDU (list)
    LISTSERV@ASUVM.INRE.ASU.EDU (listserv)

AERA-C Division C: Learning and Instruction (AERA-C)
Intended to promote the exchange of information among scholars and researchers studying learning and instruction.
    AERA-C@ASUVM.INRE.ASU.EDU (list)
    LISTSERV@ASUVM.INRE.ASU.EDU (listserv)

AERA-H Division H: School Evaluation and Program Development (AERA-H)
Intended to promote the exchange of information among scholars and researchers engaged in school evaluation and program development.
AERA-H@ASUVM.INRE.ASU.EDU (list)
LISTSERV@ASUVM.INRE.ASU.EDU (listserv)

CPT Curriculum Mailing List (CURRICUL)
CURRICUL@VM.CC.PURDUE.EDU (list)
LISTSERV@VM.CC.PURDUE.EDU (listserv)

Curriculum and Instruction Department Discussion (CANDI-L)
CANDI-L@MIZZOU1.MISSOURI.EDU (list)
LISTSERV@MIZZOU1.MISSOURI.EDU (listserv)

English / Foreign Languages

Language and Education in Lingual Setting (MULTI-L)
MULTI-L@VM.BIU.AC.IL (list)
LISTSERV@VM.BIU.AC.IL (listserv)

Foreign Language Teaching (FLTEACH)
A forum for communication among foreign language teachers at the high school and college levels.
FLTEACH@UBVM.CC.BUFFALO.EDU (list)
LISTSERV@UBVM.CC.BUFFALO.EDU (listserv)

Teaching English (ENGLISH-TEACHERS)
English-teachers is a public access list devoted to discussing matters relevant to the teaching of English, K–University.
ENGLISH-TEACHERS@UX1.CSO.UIUC.EDU (list)
MAJORDOMO@UX1.CSO.UIUC.EDU (listserv)

Teachers of English as a Second or Foreign Language to Children (TESLK-12)
Focus on issues related to younger children using English as a second language.
TESLK-12@CUNYVM.CUNY.EDU (list)
LISTSERV@CUNYVM.CUNY.EDU (listserv)

General Education Lists

A discussion list for International Educator (INTER-EU)
    INTER-EU@NIC.SURFNET.NL (list)
    LISTSERV@NIC.SURFNET.NL (listserv)

A list for primary and post-primary schools (SCHOOL-L)
    SCHOOL-L@IRLEARN.UCD.IE (list)
    LISTSERV@IRLEARN.UCD.IE (listserv)

AERA-A Division A: Administration (AERA-A)
Intended to promote the exchange of information among scholars and researchers studying educational administration.
    AERA-A@ASUVM.INRE.ASU.EDU (list)
    LISTSERV@ASUVM.INRE.ASU.EDU (listserv)

AERA-D Division D: Measurement and Research Methodology (AERA-D)
Intended to promote the exchange of information among scholars and researchers studying measurement and research methodology.
    AERA-D@ASUVM.INRE.ASU.EDU (list)
    LISTSERV@ASUVM.INRE.ASU.EDU (listserv)

AERA-E Division E: Counseling and Human Development (AERA-E)
Intended to promote the exchange of information among scholars and researchers studying counseling and human development.
    AERA-E@ASUVM.INRE.ASU.EDU (list)
    LISTSERV@ASUVM.INRE.ASU.EDU (listserv)

AERA-G Division G: Social Context of Education (AERA-G)
Intended to promote the exchange of information among scholars and researchers studying the social context of education.
    AERA-G@ASUVM.INRE.ASU.EDU (list)
    LISTSERV@ASUVM.INRE.ASU.EDU (listserv)

AERA-I Division I: Education in the Professions (AERA-I)
Intended to promote the exchange of information among scholars and researchers studying education in the professions.
    AERA-I@ASUVM.INRE.ASU.EDU (list)
    LISTSERV@ASUVM.INRE.ASU.EDU (listserv)

AERA-J Division J: Postsecondary Education (AERA-J)
Intended to promote the exchange of information among scholars and researchers studying postsecondary education.

AERA-J@ASUVM.INRE.ASU.EDU (list)
LISTSERV@ASUVM.INRE.ASU.EDU (listserv)

AERA-K Division K: Teaching and Teacher Education (AERA-K)
Intended to promote the exchange of information among scholars and researchers studying teaching and teacher education.

AERA-K@ASUVM.INRE.ASU.EDU (list)
LISTSERV@ASUVM.INRE.ASU.EDU (listserv)

American Association for Agricultural Education (AAAE)

AAAE@VM.CC.PURDUE.EDU (list)
LISTSERV@VM.CC.PURDUE.EDU (listserv)

American Association of Educational Service Agencies (AAESA-L)
An open, unmoderated discussion list on the topic of Educational Service Agencies (ESAs) throughout North America.

AAESA-L@ADMIN.ACES.K12.CT.US (list)
MAILSERV@ADMIN.ACES.K12.CT.US (listserv)

Belferon Discussion List for Teachers (BELFERON)
Belferon private discussion list is addressed to teachers, tutors, and educators. Problems discussed here are connected with education and the life of the contemporary school.

BELFERON@PLEARN.EDU.PL (list)
LISTSERV@PLEARN.EDU.PL (listserv)

Children's Rights List (Y-RIGHTS)
List on the subject of the rights of children and adolescents.

Y-RIGHTS@SJUVM.STJOHNS.EDU (list)
LISTSERV@SJUVM.STJOHNS.EDU (listserv)

CREAD Workshop on Distance Education Quality (CREAD-D)

CREAD-D@VM1.YORKU.CA (list)
LISTSERV@VM1.YORKU.CA (listserv)

Creativity and Creative Problem Solving (CREA-CPS)
For anyone interested in creative thinking and its relation to the problem-solving process.

CREA-CPS@NIC.SURFNET.NL (list)
LISTSERV@NIC.SURFNET.NL (listserv)

DEC's Education/Science Unit Monthly Newsletter (DECNEWS)
The newsletter's purpose is to provide a single, compact source of information about Digital to users in educational institutions and research organizations.

DECNEWS@UBVM.CC.BUFFALO.EDU (list)
LISTSERV@UBVM.CC.BUFFALO.EDU (listserv)

DEC's The Education Initiative Discussion List (DECTEI-L)
Created to facilitate discussion about Digital Equipment's set of education discount programs; The Education Initiative (TEI): Campus-wide Software License Grant (CSLG); Education Software Library (ESL); Education Market Basket (EMB); and others.

DECTEI-L@UBVM.CC.BUFFALO.EDU (list)
LISTSERV@UBVM.CC.BUFFALO.EDU (listserv)

Distance Education Online (DEOS-L)
DEOSNEWS is a weekly publication for professionals and students in the field of distance education.

DEOS-L@PSUVM.PSU.EDU (list)
LISTSERV@PSUVM.PSU.EDU (listserv)

Discussion on the UN Convention on the Rights of the Child (CHILDRI-L)

CHILDRI-L@NIC.SURFNET.NL (list)
LISTSERV@NIC.SURFNET.NL (listserv)

Early Childhood Education On-Line Mailing List (ECEOL-L)

ECEOL-L@MAINE.MAINE.EDU (list)
LISTSERV@MAINE.MAINE.EDU (listserv)

Early Childhood Education/Young Children (0–8) (ECENET-L)

ECENET-L@VMD.CSO.UIUC.EDU (list)
LISTSERV@POSTOFFICE.CSO.UIUC.EDU (listserv)

Education Policy Analysis Archives: An Electronic Journal (EDPOLYAR)
Publishes peer-reviewed articles of between five hundred and fifteen hundred lines in length on all aspects of education policy analysis. Submissions from the field are welcomed.

EDPOLYAR@ASUVM.INRE.ASU.EDU (list)
LISTSERV@ASUVM.INRE.ASU.EDU (listserv)

Educational Institution Networks (FORSUM-L)
The Alliance for Environmental Education is working with the US Department of Education and the White House to extend President Clinton's April 2 1995 Northwest Forest Summit in Portland, Oregon, to the K–12 and university communities via computer networks.

FORSUM-L@BROWNVM.BROWN.EDU (list)
LISTSERV@BROWNVM.BROWN.EDU (listserv)

Educational Research List (ERL-L)
  ERL-L@ASUVM.INRE.ASU.EDU (list)
  LISTSERV@ASUVM.INRE.ASU.EDU (listserv)

Edunet
Edunet is a worldwide email mailing list set up to aid in facilitating educational discussions between teachers and future teachers. It is funded by the Curriculum and Instruction Department of the College of Education at Iowa State University.
  EDUNET@IASTATE.EDU (list)
  MAJORDOMO@IASTATE.EDU (listserv)

Fiscal Issues, Policy and Education Finance (FIPEFS-L)
  FIPEFS-L@UICVM.UIC.EDU (list)
  LISTSERV@UICVM.UIC.EDU (listserv)

Forum for the Quality of Education (BGEDU-L)
  BGEDU-L@UKCC.UKY.EDU (list)
  LISTSERV@UKCC.UKY.EDU (listserv)

Institute for Educational Management List (IEM25)
  IEM25@URIACC.URI.EDU (list)
  LISTSERV@URIACC.URI.EDU (listserv)

International Curriculum (GC-L)
Intended to help American higher education find ways to accelerate the internationalization of the curriculum, in light of the rapidly globalizing daily life and the world economy.
  GC-L@URIACC.URI.EDU (list)
  LISTSERV@URIACC.URI.EDU (listserv)

Interdisciplinary Studies(INTERDIS)
  INTERDIS@MIAMIU.MUOHIO.EDU (list)
  LISTSERV@MIAMIU.MUOHIO.EDU (listserv)

K–12 School Administrator Discussion (K12ADMIN)
A worldwide discussion group for K–12 school administrators set up to provide a discussion base for K–12 school administrators: principals, vice principals, superintendents, assistant superintendents, central and county office administrators, and others involved with K–12 school administration.
  K12ADMIN@LISTSERV.SYR.EDU (list)
  LISTSERV@LISTSERV.SYR.EDU (listserv)

Law and Education (EDLAW)
For those who teach and practice law concerning public education, private education, and colleges and universities.

EDLAW@UKCC.UKY.EDU (list)
LISTSERV@UKCC.UKY.EDU (listserv)

The Learning List (LEARNING)
A forum for discussing child-centered learning.
LEARNING@SEA.EAST.SUN.COM (list)
LEARNING-REQUEST@SEA.EAST.SUN.COM (listserv)

Learning Style Movement (EDSTYLE)
Intended to help maximize teaching effectiveness by taking people's preferred styles of learning into account.
EDSTYLE@SJUVM.STJOHNS.EDU (list)
LISTSERV@SJUVM.STJOHNS.EDU (listserv)

Middle Level Education/Early Adolescence (MIDDLE-L)
MIDDLE-L@VMD.CSO.UIUC.EDU (list)
LISTSERV@VMD.CSO.UIUC.EDU (listserv)

Multicultural Education Discussion (MULTC-ED)
MULTC-ED@UMDD.BITNET (list)
LISTSERV@UMDD.BITNET (listserv)

National Association of Educational Buyers (NAEB-L)
NAEB-L@RITVM.BITNET (list)
LISTSERV@RITVM.BITNET (listserv)

Networking Lead Teachers (LEADTCHR)
LEADTCHR@PSUVM.PSU.EDU (list)
LISTSERV@PSUVM.PSU.EDU (listserv)

NRC: Teacher Education Research Study Group (TERSG-L)
TERSG-L@UBVM.CC.BUFFALO.EDU (list)
LISTSERV@UBVM.CC.BUFFALO.EDU (listserv)

Professionals and Students Discussing Education (EDPOLYAN)
Intended to be a place where people will discuss, ask questions, give answers and make their work and ideas available to their colleagues around the country.
EDPOLYAN@ASUVM.INRE.ASU.EDU (list)
LISTSERV@ASUVM.INRE.ASU.EDU (listserv)

Provide Support and Information to K–12 Teachers
LRN-ED@LISTSERV.SYR.EDU (list)
LISTSERV@LISTSERV.SYR.EDU (listserv)

School Nurse List (SCHLRN-L)
Organized for school nurses, school nurse practitioners, school nurse teachers, and school nurse managers to (1) promote networking among school nurse professionals;

(2) assist in the dissemination of research and technological advancements that would enhance the delivery of care to the student population; (3) provide a forum for the discussion of legislation, policy, and regulatory issues that affect school.
> SCHLRN-L@UBVM.CC.BUFFALO.EDU (list)
> LISTSERV@UBVM.CC.BUFFALO.EDU (listserv)

Sharing Resources for High School Physics (PHYSHARE)
> PHYSHARE@PSUVM.PSU.EDU (list)
> LISTSERV@PSUVM.PSU.EDU (listserv)

Teachers Applying Whole Language (TAWL)
> TAWL@LISTSERV.ARIZONA.EDU (list)
> LISTSERV@LISTSERV.ARIZONA.EDU (listserv)

Teachers and Student Discussions (TEACHNET)
> TEACHNET@KENTVM.KENT.EDU (list)
> LISTSERV@KENTVM.KENT.EDU (listserv)

Vocational Education Discussion (VOCNET)
VOCNET is an open, unmoderated discussion list for all who are interested in any aspect of vocational education.
> VOCNET@CMSA.BERKELEY.EDU (list)
> LISTSERV@CMSA.BERKELEY.EDU (listserv)

VT K–12 School Network (VT-HSNET)
> VT-HSNET@VTVM1.CC.VT.EDU (list)
> LISTSERV@VTVM1.CC.VT.EDU (listserv)

Home Schooling / Home Education

Home Education (HOME-ED)
This mailing list is for the discussion of all aspects and methods of home education.
> HOME-ED@THINK.COM (list)
> HOME-ED@THINK.COM (listserv)

Home Education Politics (HOME-ED-POLITICS)
Discussion of home education techniques and issues, typically by home educators.
> HOME-ED-POLITICS@MAINSTREAM.COM (list)
> HOME-ED-POLITICS-REQUEST@MAINSTREAM.COM (listserv)

Home Education Research Discussion List (HMEDRSCH)
> HMEDRSCH@ETSUADMN.ETSU.EDU (list)
> LISTSERV@ETSUADMN.ETSU.EDU (listserv)

Journalism

High School Scholastic Journalism (HSJOURN)
Anyone interested in scholastic journalism (i.e. journalism at the high school or junior high school level).
    HSJOURN@VM.CC.LATECH.EDU (list)
    LISTSERV@VM.CC.LATECH.EDU (listserv)

Kid Media Discussion List (KID.MEDIA)
Dedicated to the advancement of communications between people interested in, or involved in, the creation, production, distribution and/or consumption of media whose primary audience is children.
    KID.MEDIA@AIRWAVES.CHI.IL.US (list)
    KID.MEDIA-REQUEST@AIRWAVES.CHI.IL.US (listserv)

Kids and Listservs

International E-Mail Classroom Connections (IECC)
This mailing list serves as a meeting place for teachers seeking partner classes for international and cross-cultural electronic mail exchanges.
    IECC@STOLAF.EDU (list)
    IECC-REQUEST@STOLAF.EDU (listserv)

KIDCAFE Kids-91 Dialog
    KIDCAFE@VM1.NODAK.EDU (list)
    LISTSERV@VM1.NODAK.EDU (listserv)

KidLink Newsletter Distribution (KIDNEWS)
    KIDNEWS@VM1.NODAK.EDU (list)
    LISTSERV@VM1.NODAK.EDU (listserv)

KIDS-ACT What Can I Do
    KIDS-ACT@VM1.NODAK.EDU (list)
    LISTSERV@VM1.NODAK.EDU (listserv)

Kidzmail: Kids Exploring Issues and Interests (KIDZMAIL)
    KIDZMAIL@ASUVM.INRE.ASU.EDU (list)
    LISTSERV@ASUVM.INRE.ASU.EDU (listserv)

Response to KIDS-91
    RESPONSE@VM1.NODAK.EDU (list)
    LISTSERV@VM1.NODAK.EDU (listserv)

Room 13's Question of the Week (RM13-L)
A chance for students and classrooms to share their thoughts and opinions on the world, their lives, and their hopes.
RM13-L@TELEPORT.COM (list)
MAJORDOMO@TELEPORT.COM (listserv)

Language Arts and Literature

Children's Literature: Criticism and Theory (CHILDLIT)
    CHILDLIT@RUTVM1.RUTGERS.EDU (list)
    LISTSERV@RUTVM1.RUTGERS.EDU (listserv)

Children and Youth Literature List (KIDLIT)
    KIDLIT-L@BINGVMB.CC.BINGHAMTON.EDU (list)
    LISTSERV@BINGVMB.CC.BINGHAMTON.EDU (listserv)

Creative Writing Pedagogy for Teachers and Students (CREWRT-L)
This list was created as a place to discuss how and why creative writing is being taught at colleges and universities, including the role it plays in the curriculum, the history of creative writing programs, the shape and flavor of creative writing courses, and the influence it has or should have on students' lives. For any teacher who has ever taught a creative writing course (poetry or fiction) and any student who has ever taken such a course.
    CREWRT-L@UMCVMB.MISSOURI.EDU (list)
    LISTSERV@UMCVMB.MISSOURI.EDU (listserv)

Dead Teachers Society Discussion List (DTS-L)
    DTS-L@IUBVM.UCS.INDIANA.EDU (list)
    LISTSERV@IUBVM.UCS.INDIANA.EDU (listserv)

Literacy (LITERACY)
A moderated general discussion group for individuals concerned with the issues of literacy.
    LITERACY@NYSERNET.ORG (list)
    LISTSERV@NYSERNET.ORG (listserv)

Writing Across the Curriculum
    WAC-L@VMD.CSO.UIUC.EDU (list)
    LISTSERV@POSTOFFICE.CSO.UIUC.EDU (listserv)

Math

Creativity and Creative Problem Solving (CREA-CPS)
For anyone interested in creative thinking and its relation to the problem-solving process.
    CREA-CPS@NIC.SURFNET.NL (list)
    LISTSERV@NIC.SURFNET.NL (listserv)

Family Math (FAM-MATH)
    FAM-MATH@UICVM.UIC.EDU (list)
    LISTSERV@UICVM.UIC.EDU (listserv)

Institute for Math and Science Education (MSE-L)
    IMSE-L@UICVM.UIC.EDU (list)
    LISTSERV@UICVM.UIC.EDU (listserv)

Math Magic (MATHMAGIC-GENERAL-OPEN)
A K–12 project that provides a strong motivation for students to use computer technology while increasing problem-solving strategies and communications skills. To find out more information about the mathmagic program, send email to the listserv with "info mathmagic-general-open" in the body of your message.
    MATHMAGIC-K-3-OPEN@FORUM.SWARTHMORE.EDU (list)
    MATHMAGIC-K-3@FORUM.SWARTHMORE.EDU (list)
    MATHMAGIC-4-6-OPEN@FORUM.SWARTHMORE.EDU (list)
    MATHMAGIC-4-6@FORUM.SWARTHMORE.EDU (list)
    MATHMAGIC-7-9-OPEN@FORUM.SWARTHMORE.EDU (list)
    MATHMAGIC-7-9@FORUM.SWARTHMORE.EDU (list)
    MATHMAGIC-10-12-OPEN@FORUM.SWARTHMORE.EDU (list)
    MATHMAGIC-10-12@FORUM.SWARTHMORE.EDU (list)
    MATHMAGIC-GENERAL-OPEN@FORUM.SWARTHMORE.EDU
      (list)
    MAJORDOMO@FORUM.SWARTHMORE.EDU (listserv)

Math Science Upward Bound Discussion List (MSUPBND)
Forum for those interested in the Math Science Upward Bound program.
    MSUPBND@UBVM.CC.BUFFALO.EDU (list)
    LISTSERV@UBVM.CC.BUFFALO.EDU (listserv)

The Technology in Mathematics Education (MATHEDCC)
    MATHEDCC@VM1.MCGILL.CA (list)
    LISTSERV@VM1.MCGILL.CA (listserv)

Media and Education

AEMA-L: Arizona Educational Media Association
   AEMA-L@ASUVM.INRE.ASU.EDU (list)
   LISTSERV@ASUVM.INRE.ASU.EDU (listserv)

A Discussion Group For California Library Media Teachers (CALIBK12)
Set up to serve the school library media community in California.
CALIBK12@SJSUVM1.SJSU.EDU (list)
LISTSERV@SJSUVM1.SJSU.EDU (listserv)

Media in Education (MEDIA-L)
For people in the media services profession who would like to share information or ask questions about educational communications and technology issues.
   MEDIA-L@BINGVMB.CC.BINGHAMTON.EDU (list)
   LISTSERV@BINGVMB.CC.BINGHAMTON.EDU (listserv)

School Library Media People (LM_NET)
Set up to serve the school library media community, worldwide.
   LM_NET@LISTSERV.SYR.EDU (list)
   LISTSERV@LISTSERV.SYR.EDU (listserv)

Music

Music Education (MUSIC-ED)
   MUSIC-ED@VM1.SPCS.UMN.EDU (list)
   LISTSERV@VM1.SPCS.UMN.EDU (listserv)

Project-Oriented

International E-Mail Classroom Connections (IECC)
This mailing list serves as a meeting place for teachers seeking partner classes for international and cross-cultural electronic mail exchanges.
   IECC@STOLAF.EDU (list)
   IECC-REQUEST@STOLAF.EDU (listserv)

Project Introducing for Children in Project (KIDINTRO)
   KIDINTRO@SJUVM.STJOHNS.EDU (list)
   LISTSERV@SJUVM.STJOHNS.EDU (listserv)

Students

(...EMORIES)

)

(...VIEW)

)

(...ECAP)

)

)

(GALILEO)

MAJORDOMO@UNR.EDU (listserv)

Insect Education (BUGNET)
    BUGNET@WSUVM1.CSC.WSU.EDU (list)
    LISTSERV@WSUVM1.CSC.WSU.EDU (listserv)

Marine Scientists—High School Student Exchange (FISH-JUNIOR)
A forum for knowledge transfer between marine scientists and children/high school students.
    FISH-JUNIOR@SEARN.SUNET.SE (list)
    LISTSERV@SEARN.SUNET.SE (listserv)

NASA Classroom of the Future (T3-L)
    T3-L@WVNVM.WVNET.EDU (list)
    LISTSERV@WVNVM.WVNET.EDU (listserv)

Secondary Biology Teacher Enhancement (PIBIOPI-L)
    BIOPI-L@KSUVM.KSU.EDU (list)
    LISTSERV@KSUVM.KSU.EDU (listserv)

Teaching Science in Elementary Schools (T321-L)
    T321-L@MIZZOU1.MISSOURI.EDU (list)
    LISTSERV@MIZZOU1.MISSOURI.EDU (listserv)

Teaching Science Labs Via Distance
DISTLABS@MIAMIU.MUOHIO.EDU (list)
LISTSERV@MIAMIU.MUOHIO.EDU (listserv)

Social Studies / Global Studies

AERA-F Division F: History and Historiography (AERA-F)
Intended to promote the exchange of information among scholars and researchers studying history and historiography.
AERA-F@ASUVM.INRE.ASU.EDU (list)
LISTSERV@ASUVM.INRE.ASU.EDU (listserv)

Education Issues in Geography (GEOGED)
This list is open to the discussion of all topics relating to education issues in geography.
GEOGED@UKCC.UKY.EDU (list)
LISTSERV@UKCC.UKY.EDU (listserv)

Educational Needs of Indigenous Peoples (NAT-EDU)
A moderated list for exchanging information and ideas about topics relating to the educational needs of any of the world's indigenous peoples (the original inhabitants of particular geographical regions).
NAT-EDU@INDYCMS.IUPUI.EDU (list)
NAT-EDU-REQUEST@INDYCMS.IUPUI.EDU (listserv)

School Management (SCHOOL-MANAGEMENT)
Discussion of education in schools, in particular their management and government and the curriculum.
SCHOOL-MANAGEMENT@MAILBASE.AC.UK (list)
MAILBASE@MAILBASE.AC.UK (listserv)

The Today Mailing List (TODAY)
Daily list of historical events and famous birthdays.
TODAY@POBOX.COM (list)
MAJORDOMO@POBOX.COM (listserv)

Special Needs Students and Learning Conditions

Behavioral and Emotional Disorders in Children (BEHAVIOR)
BEHAVIOR@ASUVM.INRE.ASU.EDU (list)
LISTSERV@ASUVM.INRE.ASU.EDU (listserv)

Children with Special Health Care Needs (CSHCN-L)
    CSHCN-L@NERVM.NERDC.UFL.EDU (list)
    LISTSERV@NERVM.NERDC.UFL.EDU (listserv)

SPAPT:Deaf-Blind Discussion List (DEAFBLND)
The mission of DEAFBLND is to share information, inquiries, ideas, and opinions on matters pertaining to dual sensory impairment.
    DEAFBLND@UKCC.UKY.EDU (list)
    LISTSERV@UKCC.UKY.EDU (listserv)

Developmentally Disabled and Autism (AUTISM)
Devoted to the developmentally disabled and autistic. Its purpose is to provide a forum for those who are developmentally disabled, their teachers, and those interested in this area.
    AUTISM@SJUVM.STJOHNS.EDU (list)
    LISTSERV@SJUVM.STJOHNS.EDU (listserv)

Discussion of Topics in Special Education (SPEDTALK)
A forum for people to discuss current issues about practices, policies, and research in special education.
    SPEDTALK@VIRGINIA.EDU (list)
    MAJORDOMO@VIRGINIA.EDU (listserv)

Gifted Education (GIFTEDNET-L)
Information exchange pertaining to research, curriculum, intellectual, academic, moral and ethical, social, and emotional needs of gifted learners.
    GIFTEDNET-L@LISTSERV.CC.WM.EDU (list)
    LISTSERVER@LISTSERV.CC.WM.EDU (listserv)

ICIDH Revisions—Childhood Impairment (DS-C-IMP)
Overview forum discussing spina bifida and cerebral palsy.
    DS-C-IMP@LIST.NIH.GOV (list)
    LISTSERV@LIST.NIH.GOV (listserv)

L-HCAP List (L-HCAP)
Discussion of issues related to handicapped people in education.
    L-HCAP@VM1.NODAK.EDU (list)
    LISTSERV@VM1.NODAK.EDU (listserv)

Technology and Education

AAHE Info. Tech. Activities & Projects (AAHESGIT)
    AHESGIT@GWUVM.GWU.EDU (list)
    LISTSERV@GWUVM.GWU.EDU (listserv)

AERA SIG/ENET Discussion (ENET-L)
The primary purpose of the list is to facilitate discussion among educators and educational researchers interested in information technology and attendant resources.
> ENET-L@UHCCVM.UHCC.HAWAII.EDU (list)
> LISTSERV@UHCCVM.UHCC.HAWAII.EDU (listserv)

Apple Education Consultants Program (AECP)
> AECP-L@UNBVM1.CSD.UNB.CA (list)
> LISTSERV@UNBVM1.CSD.UNB.CA (listserv)

Computers in Physics Education (CIPE-L)
> CIPE-L@UWF.CC.UWF.EDU (list)
> LISTSERV@UWF.CC.UWF.EDU (listserv)

Computer Graphics Education Newsletter (CGE)
> CGE@VM.MARIST.EDU (list)
> LISTSERV@VM.MARIST.EDU (listserv)

Equal Access to Software and Information (EASI)
Serves as a resource primarily to the education community by providing information and guidance in the area of access-to-information technologies by persons with disabilities.
> EASI@SJUVM.STJOHNS.EDU (list)
> LISTSERV@SJUVM.STJOHNS.EDU (listserv)

Educational Computing and Instructional Development (ECID-L)
> ECID-L@VM.CC.PURDUE.EDU (list)
> LISTSERV@VM.CC.PURDUE.EDU (listserv)

High Performance Internet & Computer Apps in K–12 (SUPERK12)
> SUPERK12@LISTSERV.SYR.EDU (list)
> LISTSERV@LISTSERV.SYR.EDU (listserv)

Hypertext in Education (HYPEREDU)
The purpose of the list is to promote a discussion about use of hypertexts and hypermedia in education and in particular the advantages versus disadvantages of the introduction of these tools at any educational level (from elementary school to college).
> HYPEREDU@ITOCSIVM.CSI.IT (list)
> LISTSERV@ITOCSIVM.CSI.IT (listserv)

Internet Access for K–12 Discussions (WVNK12)
> WVNK12-L@WVNVM.WVNET.EDU (list)
> LISTSERV@WVNVM.WVNET.EDU (listserv)

Internet Navigation Course for K–12 Educators (K12NAV-L)
    K12NAV-L@KENTVM.KENT.EDU (list)
    LISTSERV@KENTVM.KENT.EDU (listserv)

Kidsphere (KIDSPHERE)
Established in 1989 to facilitate the international development of a computer network for children and their teachers.
    KIDSPHERE@VMS.CIS.PITT.EDU (list)
    LISTSERV@VMS.CIS.PITT.EDU (listserv)

Kindergarten. Primary & Secondary School Computing (KIDSNET)
Provides a global network for use by children and teachers in grades K–12. It is intended to provide a focus for technological development and for resolving the problems of language, standards, etc. that inevitably arise in international communications.
    KIDSNET@VMS.CIS.PITT.EDU (list)
    KIDSNET-REQUEST@VMS.CIS.PITT.EDU (listserv)

Networking Lead Teachers (LEADTCHR)
    LEADTCHR@PSUVM.PSU.EDU (list)
    LISTSERV@PSUVM.PSU.EDU (listserv)

Novae Group Teachers Networking for the Future (NOVAE)
Novae provides list subscribers with a weekly newsletter highlighting educational sites on the Internet. From World Wide Web addresses to new listservs, classroom projects, and grant announcements, the Novae Group provides a newsletter for all teachers.
    NOVAE@IDBSU.IDBSU.EDU (list)
    LISTSERV@IDBSU.IDBSU.EDU (listserv)

RuralNet Discussion Group (WVRK12-L)
    WVRK12-L@WVNVM.WVNET.EDU (list)
    LISTSERV@WVNVM.WVNET.EDU (listserv)

Use of Networks in Education (EDNET)
A Massachusetts list for those interested in exploring the educational potential of the Internet.
    EDNET@NIC.UMASS.EDU (list)
    LISTSERV@LISTS.UMASS.EDU (listserv)

Using Computers to Learn (CTI-L)
Unmoderated list to facilitate the discussion of issues in the use of computers in teaching.
    CTI-L@IRLEARN.UCD.IE (list)
    LISTSERV@IRLEARN.UCD.IE (listserv)

Newsgroups of Interest to Teachers and Students

Art and Music

k12.ed.art   Art curriculum in K–12 education.

k12.ed.music   Music curriculum in K–12 education.

rec.arts.marching.band.high-school   High school marching bands.

uiuc.org.music-ed   Music education discussions.

Chat Groups

alt.kids.talk   A place for the pre-college set on the net.

aus.students   Going to school in Australia?

k12.chat.elementary   Informal discussion among elementary students, grades K–5.

k12.chat.junior   Informal discussion among students in grades 6–8.

k12.chat.senior   Informal discussion among high school students.

k12.chat.teacher   Informal discussion among teachers of K–12 education.

nptn.teacher.aone-prog   NPTN Teacher group (moderated).

nptn.teacher.cityyouth   Discussion area for school and community problems of teachers (moderated).

nptn.teacher.ide-discuss   NPTN discussion for teachers (moderated).

nptn.teacher.professional   NPTN teacher professional group (moderated).

rec.arts.books.childrens   Discussion about children's literature.

rec.arts.marching.band.high-school   High school marching bands.

schl.call.general   Keypals, sister schools, and informal projects.

schl.kids.kidcafe   Discussion forum for KidCafe (ages 10–15 only) (moderated).

schl.sig.k12admin   K–12 School administrators discussion group (moderated).

schl.stu.elem   Elementary Keypals (moderated).

schl.stu.high   High school Keypals (moderated).

schl.stu.hobbies   Talk about your hobbies (moderated).

schl.stu.issues   Discussion on important issues related to education (moderated).

schl.stu.jrhi   Middle school Keypals (moderated).

schl.stu.news   Share campus, local, and regional news and events (moderated).

schl.stu.sports   Discuss your favorite sports and teams (moderated).

uk.education.teachers   For discussion by/about teachers, United Kingdom.

English as a Second Language and Foreign Language Education

bit.listserv.tesl-l   Teachers of ESL Listserv (moderated).

k12.lang.deutsch-eng   Bilingual German/English practice with native speakers.

k12.lang.esp-eng   Bilingual Spanish/English practice with native speakers.

k12.lang.francais   Bilingual French/English practice with native speakers.

k12.lang.russian   Bilingual Russian/English practice with native speakers.

misc.education.language.english   Teaching English to speakers of other languages.

schl.call.orillas   de Orilla a Orilla: en español y francais (moderated).

uiuc.class.eil367   Communicative approaches to second and foreign language teaching.

uiuc.class.eil371   Teaching composition in the ESL classroom.

uiuc.class.human279   Introduction to foreign language education.

uiuc.class.human382   Computer-based foreign language teaching.

uiuc.class.span274   Spanish grammar for communicative language teaching.

General Education Discussions

alt.education.distance   Learning over networks.

aus.education   Helping educators in Australia.

aus.education.open-learning   Open learning education in Australia.

aus.students   Going to school in Australia?

bit.listserv.aera   American Educational Research Association.

bit.listserv.edpolyan   Education policy analysis forum listserv (moderated).

clari.news.education   Primary and secondary education (moderated).

clari.news.education.higher   Colleges and universities (moderated).

fj.education   About education in general in Fiji.

misc.education   Discussion of the educational system.

misc.kids.info   Informational posts related to misc.kids.hierarchy (moderated).

nptn.academy.teacher.tips   Academy One tips for teachers (moderated).

nptn.student.cityyouth   Discussion area for school and community problems of students (moderated).

nptn.student.school-sig   NPTN student special interest group (moderated).

nptn.teacher.cityyouth   Discussion area for school and community problems of teachers (moderated).

nptn.teacher.ide-discuss   NPTN discussion for teachers (moderated).

nptn.teacher.jewish-ed   NPTN Jewish education (moderated).

nptn.teacher.msn   NPTN msn teacher group (moderated).

nptn.teacher.pat-discussion   NPTN pat discussion group (moderated).

nptn.teacher.pcg-events   NPTN pcg events posted (moderated).

nptn.teacher.pcg-reports   NPTN pcg reports posted from events (moderated).

nptn.teacher.professional   NPTN teacher professional group (moderated).

pnet.school.k-12   Discussion about K–12 education.

pnet.school.k-5   Discussion about K–5 education.

pnet.school.pta   Parent-Teacher Association discussion group.

relcom.education   Education discussions.

schl.call.general   Key pals, sister schools, and informal projects.

schl.news.cnn   CNN Newsroom lesson plans (moderated).

schl.news.edupage   Educom's trice weekly EDUPAGE Newsletter (moderated).

schl.news.nethappen   Gleason Sackman's Internet NetHappenings (moderated).

schl.news.reportcard   America 2000 daily report card (moderated).

schl.news.urban-ed   ERIC urban ed news reports (moderated).

schl.sig.ethics   Discuss character/ethics/morals of education (moderated).

schl.sig.k12admin   K–12 school administrators discussion group (moderated).

schl.sig.satl-con   Satellite conferences with Secretary of Education (moderated).

schl.stu.issues   Discussion on important issues related to education (moderated).

schl.stu.news   Share campus, local, and regional news and events (moderated).

uiuc.class.c+i240   Secondary education in the United States.

uiuc.class.c+i321   Principles and practices in early childhood education.

uk.education.misc   General discussion on education, United Kingdom.

uk.education.teachers   For discussion by/about teachers, United Kingdom.

za.schools   Issues affecting primary and secondary education.

Health and Physical Education

fj.life.children   Children, childcare, and parenting.

k12.ed.health-pe   Health and physical education curriculum in grades K–12.

misc.kids   Children, their behavior, and activities.

misc.kids.health   Children's health issues.

nptn.clinic.child-psych   Child psychology clinic from NPTN (moderated).

nptn.teacher.ped-illness   NPTN pediatric illnesses (moderated).

uiuc.class.edpsy211   Educational psychology.

Home Schooling

misc.education.home-school.christian   Christian home-schooling discussion.

misc.education.home-school.misc   General discussion about home-schooling.

schl.sig.home-ed   Discussion of home-schooling topics and problems (moderated).

Language Arts

k12.lang.art   Language arts curriculum in K–12 education.

rec.arts.books.childrens   Discussion about children's literature.

schl.call.english   Language arts project announcements (moderated).

schl.proj.writing   Publish your students' writing (moderated).

schl.stu.author   Share stories, poems, and articles (moderated).

schl.stu.reviews   Discussion and review of books, music, TV, and movies (moderated).

uiuc.class.c+i370   Principles and practices in reading education.

Mathematics

alt.calc-reform   Discussions of alternate ways to teach calculus.

fj.education.math   Discussions on mathematics education.

k12.ed.math   Mathematics curriculum in K–12 education.

schl.call.mathsci   Math and science project announcements (moderated).

schl.proj.mathmagic   Math problem-solving activities (moderated).

schl.stu.puzzles   Post and solve puzzles and brainteasers (moderated).

uiuc.class.c+i430   Trends and issues in mathematics education.

Project Discussion Groups

k12.sys.channel0   Project Channel 0.

k12.sys.channel1   Project Channel 1.

k12.sys.channel10   Project Channel 10.

k12.sys.channel11   Project Channel 11.

k12.sys.channel12   Project Channel 12.

k12.sys.channel2   Project Channel 2.

k12.sys.channel3   Project Channel 3.

k12.sys.channel4   Project Channel 4.

k12.sys.channel5   Project Channel 5.

k12.sys.channel6   Project Channel 6.

k12.sys.channel7   Project Channel 7.

k12.sys.channel8   Project Channel 8.

k12.sys.channel9   Project Channel 9.

k12.sys.projects   Coordination of projects that use k12.sys channelN.

schl.call.english   Language arts project announcements (moderated).

schl.call.espbbs   Announcements from the European School Projects BBS.

schl.call.general   Keypals, sister schools, and informal projects.

schl.call.ideas   General project calls and announcements (moderated).

schl.call.mathsci   Math and science project announcements (moderated).

schl.gsh.discuss   Talk about your own GSH program/ask about GSH (moderated).

schl.gsh.watch   News from the Global SchoolHouse (moderated).

schl.jason.news   News from the Jason Science projects (moderated).

schl.jason.stu   Jason Project student forum (moderated).

schl.jason.teach   Jason Project teacher forum (moderated).

schl.jason.teach   Jason Project teacher forum (moderated).

schl.kids.kidcafe   Discussion forum for KidCafe (ages 10–15 only) (moderated).

schl.kids.kidforum   Topical exchanges (moderated).

schl.kids.kidleadr   Kidlink leaders forum (moderated).

schl.kids.kidlink   Kidlink announcements (moderated).

schl.kids.kidplan   Kidlink planning forum (moderated).

schl.kids.kidproj   Kidlink kid projects (moderated).

schl.kids.response   Answer four Kidlink questions here (moderated).

schl.mesaverde.preserve   Preservation and conservation projects, issues, and ideas (moderated).

schl.proj.channel1   Conduct your project here: info@acme.fred.org (moderated).

schl.proj.channel2   Conduct your project here: info@acme.fred.org (moderated).

schl.proj.channel3   Conduct your project here: info@acme.fred.org (moderated).

schl.proj.channel4   Conduct your project here: info@acme.fred.org (moderated).

schl.proj.fieldtrips   Publish your field trip reports and stories (moderated).

schl.proj.hilites   Classic project summaries and Hilites (moderated).

schl.proj.jnorth-news   Information and news regarding Journey North Project (moderated).

schl.proj.jnorth-talk   Discussion and sharing of the Journey North Project (moderated).

schl.proj.mathmagic   Math problem-solving activities (moderated).

schl.proj.newsday   The popular NEWSDAY Newswire Project (moderated).

schl.proj.research   Publish your students' research reports (moderated).

schl.proj.stars   GSN/University of Song Stars in Cyberspace Project (moderated).

schl.proj.writing   Publish your students' writing (moderated).

schl.sig.chatback   International projects for disabled children (moderated).

schl.sig.kidsphere   Kidsphere discussions from Internet (moderated).

schl.stu.projects   Projects, polls, surveys, and test (moderated).

Science

aus.education.bio-newtech   New technologies in biology teaching.

comp.lang.logo   The Logo teaching and learning language.

k12.ed.science   Science curriculum in K–12 education.

misc.education.science   Issues related to science education.

schl.call.mathsci   Math and science project announcements (moderated).

schl.call.socsci   Social science project announcements (moderated).

schl.mesaverde.archaeology   Archaeology projects, news, and topics (moderated).

schl.proj.geogame   The ever-popular Geogame Project (moderated).

schl.proj.ggl   Global Grocery List Project (moderated).

schl.proj.jnorth-news   Information and news regarding Journey North Project (moderated).

schl.proj.jnorth-talk   Discussion and sharing of the Journey North Project (moderated).

schl.proj.maya-lessons   Lesson plans and guides regarding Mayaquest Project (moderated).

schl.proj.maya-news   Information and news regarding Mayaquest Project (moderated).

schl.proj.maya-talk   Discussion and sharing regarding Mayaquest Project.

schl.proj.roger   Where on the Globe is Roger project (moderated).

schl.sig.logo   Discussion on Logo and Logowriter (moderated).

uiuc.class.c+i340   Principles and practices in science education.

Social Studies

k12.ed.soc-studies   Social studies and history curriculum in K–12 education.

misc.kids.consumers   Products related to kids.

schl.call.socsci   Social science project announcements (moderated).

schl.mesaverde.archaeology   Archaeology projects, news, and topics (moderated).

schl.mesaverde.indigenous   Native American and indigenous cultures, history, and art (moderated).

schl.proj.geogame   The ever-popular Geogame Project (moderated).

schl.proj.ggl   Global Grocery List Project (moderated).

schl.proj.jnorth-news   Information and news regarding Journey North Project (moderated).

schl.proj.jnorth-talk   Discussion and sharing of the Journey North Project (moderated).

schl.proj.maya-lessons   Lesson plans and guides regarding Mayaquest Project (moderated).

schl.proj.maya-news   Information and news regarding Mayaquest Project (moderated).

schl.proj.maya-talk   Discussion and sharing regarding Mayaquest Project.

schl.proj.roger   Where on the Globe is Roger project (moderated).

Special Needs and TAG Education

alt.education.disabled   Education issues facing the disabled.

bit.listserv.dsshe-l   Disabled student services in higher education.

k12.ed.special   K–12 education for students with handicaps or special needs.

k12.ed.tag   K–12 education for talented and gifted students.

schl.sig.chatback   International projects for disabled children (moderated).

schl.sig.tag   Discussion on talented and gifted programs (moderated).

Technology

alt.education.distance   Learning over networks.

aus.education.bio-newtech   New technologies in biology teaching.

bit.listserv.aect-l   Educational communication and technology listserv.

bit.listserv.dectei-l   DECUS education software library discussions listserv.

bit.listserv.edtech   EDTECH educational technology listserv.

bit.listserv.ibm-hesc   IBM higher education consortium.

clari.nb.education   Computers in education.

comp.edu   Computer science education.

k12.ed.comp.literacy   Teaching computer literacy in grades K–12.

k12.ed.tech   Industrial arts and vocational education in grades K–12.

misc.education.multimedia   Multimedia for education.

misc.kids.computer   The use of computers by children.

schl.call.espbbs   Announcements from the European School Projects BBS.

schl.sig.cosn   CoSN: Consortium on School Networking (moderated).

schl.sig.edtech   Discuss ed technology (moderated).

schl.sig.lmnet   LM NET: Library/Media services discussion (moderated).

schl.sig.logo   Discussion on Logo and Logowriter (moderated).

schl.sig.mmedia   Discussion on Multimedia in your classroom (moderated).

schl.stu.ascii-art   Post ASCII art here (moderated).

uiuc.class.edpsy199f   Computer education for peer educators.

uiuc.class.edpsy387   Computer use in education.

uiuc.class.human382   Computer based foreign language teaching.

uiuc.class.math200   Computers for elementary teachers.

uiuc.org.hied-hitech   High technology applications in higher education.

za.edu.comp   Discussions on the use of computer in education.

Vocational Arts

bit.listserv.covnet   Vocational education discussion group.

k12.ed.business   Business education curriculum in K–12 education.

k12.ed.life-skills   Home economics and career education in grades K–12.

k12.ed.tech   Industrial arts and vocational education in grades K–12.

uiuc.class.votec388   Special techniques of teaching career, occupational, and practical arts education.

uiuc.class.votec399   Issues and developments in vocational and technical education.

uiuc.class.votec4453   Disciplined inquiry in vocational education.

uiuc.class.votec450   Evaluation in vocational, technical, and practical arts education.

FTP Sites of Interest to Teachers and Students

Education and the Internet

Some of the following FTP sites contain files with information regarding various aspects of the Internet in general. Others are specific to education and the Internet. All can be helpful for the novice user who wishes to learn more about the Internet and how it relates to education.

FTP Site: The CNIDR FTP Server
FTP Address: ftp.cnidr.org
Directory: /pub/K12
Description: An interesting study done of students and their use of on-line media searches can be found here entitled "Media_Automation.txt".

FTP Site: Dana FTP Server
FTP Address: ftp.dana.edu
Directory: /pub/educ
Description: Various text files on the Internet and education can be found in this directory. "ftpsites.txt", "telnsite.txt", and "listserv.txt" are three such files that contain information on FTP sites, telnet sites, and listservs that are of interest to educators.

FTP Site: Electronic Frontier Foundation Library Online
FTP Address: ftp.eff.org

Directory: /pub
Description: This site can provide you with information on the Internet, growth of the Internet, rights, laws, censorship issues, etc. Download the file "00-Index.pub" for more information on specific directories and files.

FTP Site: Hydra
FTP Address: hydra.uwo.ca
Directory: /libsoft
Description: Many Internet help files can be found on this site in text format. From a guide to retrieving binary files for Usenet Newsgroups to an on-line Library resources, this site can be very helpful to the novice Internet user.

FTP Site: The K12 Net: International Educational Network
FTP Address: ftp.psg.com
Directory: /pub/k12/k12_info
Description: Information in text files can be found in this directory about the K12 Net project channels on Usenet Newsgroups.

FTP Site: Michigan State University Anonymous FTP Service
FTP Address: ftp.msu.edu
Directory: /pub/education
Description: This site contains a 1.5 megabyte text file called "Internet_&_Ed3". It is a document on the Internet and education.

FTP Site: The National Center for Technology Planning at the Mississippi State University
FTP Address: ftp.msstate.edu
Directory: /pub/archives/nctp
Description: Teachers, schools, and districts putting together a technology plan will be interested in visiting this site, which contains information on technology planning. You can also find and download examples of district wide plans and planning aids.

FTP Site: NCSA's Education Group
FTP Address: ftp.ncsa.uiuc.edu

Directory: /Education
Description: Various files on education and the Internet can be found. Look into the directory "Education_Resources", where you will find the "Incomplete Guide to the Internet."

FTP Site: SuperNet FTP Server
FTP Address: ftp.csn.net
Directory: /k12/tutorials
Description: The directory "/k12/tutorials" is a great resource for information on using the Internet in an educational setting.

FTP Site: Sydney University Law School FTP Archive, Sydney, Australia
FTP Address: sulaw.law.su.oz.au
Directory: /pub/law
Description: This archive contains information regarding computer laws and the Internet.

FTP Site: Virginia Tech Computing Center Anonymous FTP
FTP Address: ftp.vt.edu
Directory: /pub/k12
Description: Information on the Kidlink Newsgroups and Project channels.

FTP Site: University of Massachusetts
FTP Address: nic.umass.edu
Directory: /pub/ednet
Description: Educators will be interested in the file "educatrs.lst", a guide to listserv for educators.

FTP Site: US Department of Education Anonymous FTP Archives
FTP Address: ftp.ed.gov
Directory: /gopher
Description: A wealth of information from the Department of Education can be found at this site. Download a copy of the "00-INDEX" file for more information on the contents of specific directories.

Electronic Texts

Complete literary works such as *Alice and Wonderland*, *Moby Dick*, and many more can be found on the following archives.

FTP Site:	Gatekeeper
FTP Address:	gatekeeper.dec.com
Directories:	/pub
	/pub/data/gutenberg
	/pub/data/Shakespeare
Description:	Project Gutenberg, "pub/data/gutenberg", contains electronic texts of many classic books and stories including *Alice in Wonderland*, *Through the Looking Glass*, *Moby Dick*, and many more. Shakespeare is also well represented on this site in the directory "pub/data/Shakespeare".

FTP Site:	University of Saskatchewan FTP Server
FTP Address:	ftp.usask.ca
Directory:	/pub/texts
Description:	Copies of electronic articles, books, magazines, and journals. Literary works of all kinds are separated by theme.

FTP Site:	UUNET Archives, UUNET Technologies Inc.
FTP Address:	ftp.uu.net
Directory:	/doc/literary/obi
Description:	Many literary works ranging from the Gutenberg project to text documents on the Internet and electronic books by Mark Twain.

History

Much like electronic texts, these sites archive historical documents and speeches from around the world.

FTP Site:	History Network Resources
FTP Address:	ftp2.cc.ukans.edu

Directories: /pub/history
Description: Historical documents from Asia and Europe.

FTP Site: Mississippi State University's FTP Server
FTP Address: ftp.msstate.edu
Directory: /pub/docs/history
Description: A large number of historical text documents on many coun-
                tries, from Asia to the USA. Includes constitutions, famous
                speeches, and declarations.
FTP Site: Spies Archive
FTP Address: ftp.spies.com
Directory: /pub/gov/US-History
                /pub/gov/US-Speeches
Description: History texts and copies of famous speeches in United States
                history.

FTP Site: UUNET Archives, UUNET Technologies Inc.
FTP Address: ftp.uu.net
Directory: /doc/literary/obi/History
Description: Historical documents galore.

Images

The follow FTP sites contain images that can be downloaded to your machine and then viewed by using a graphic software program. In most cases
these files are in JPG format, the most common graphic format used on the
Internet. A shareware image viewer can be found in any of the "Shareware
and Freeware Archives."

FTP Site: Center of Resources and Information, Rennes University,
                France
FTP Address: ftp.univ-rennes1.fr
Directory: /pub/Images
Description: Images are arranged by category. Many to choose from and
                most in JPG and GIF formats.

FTP Site: Mexico Tech's FTP Site

FTP Address: ftp.nmt.edu
Directory: /pub/graphics
Description: Various graphic images including movies, animals, music im-
                   ages, people, space, and more can be found in JPG format.

FTP Site: Washington University Archive in St. Louis
FTP Address: wuarchive.wustl.edu
Directory: /pub/graphics
Description: Various images on many subjects in JPG format.

FTP Site: Zee-Archive
FTP Address: ftp.elvis.ru
Directory: /pub/images/animals
Description: Animal images of all kinds in JPG format.

Lesson Plans via FTP

Lesson plans on various topics available by way of FTP can be found here.

FTP Site: NASA Jet Propulsion Laboratory's public information FTP
                   archive
FTP Address: ftp.jpl.nasa.gov
Directory: /pub/educator
Description: Various science lessons.

FTP Site: SuperNet FTP Server
FTP Address: ftp.csn.net
Directory: /k12/lessons/bigsky
Description: Hundreds of lesson plans covering a large range of educa-
                   tional topics. Lessons are categorized by discipline. A great
                   place to start an educator's search for enrichment ideas and
                   lesson plans.

Music

This site contains a large archive of music lyrics, from the classics to the
modern. A music teacher's and teenager's dream site.

FTP Site: Lyrics & Discography
FTP Address: ftp.uwp.edu
Directory: /pub/music
Description: This archive of song lyrics, musical demos, guitar chords, and music history is bound to be a hit with music teachers and students alike.

Science

FTP sites relating to science concepts, geography, and weather.

FTP Site: Florida State University Meteorology Department
FTP Address: ftp.met.fsu.edu
Directory: /pub/weather/Education/EXPLORERS!
Description: Earth science teachers in primary and secondary schools will find this bibliography of references useful.

FTP Site: German National Research Center for Information Technology
FTP Address: ftp.gmd.de
Directory: /images/\satellite
Description: Weather and polar satellite images from space satellites. Most in JPG format.

FTP Site: NCSA's Education Group
FTP Address: ftp.ncsa.uiuc.edu
Directory: /Weather
Description: Weather images and classroom ideas about weather and science.

FTP Site: Stanford University
FTP Address: sepftp.stanford.edu
Directory: /pub
Description: Contained in this directory you will find directories that deal with Earth, astronomy, topography, and geology. This site offers images of Earth from space, a map database, topography information, and information that is of interest to Earth scientists.

FTP Site: The University of New Brunswick
FTP Address: jupiter.sun.csd.unb.ca
Directory: /pub/Weather.maps
Description: Weather images can be found in this directory in the JPG
                format. These files can be downloaded to your machine and
                viewed with a graphics program. Get the file "readme" for
                more information.

FTP Site: Zee-Archive
FTP Address: ftp.elvis.ru
Directory: /pub/images/animals
Description: Animal images of all kinds in JPG format.

Shareware and Freeware Archives

The following archives contain shareware and freeware programs for Mac-
intosh-, PC-, and UNIX-based machines. Programs cover a gamut of subjects from multimedia to graphics, games, educational programs, Internet
programs and software, and much, much more.

FTP Site: Anonymous FTP Server of Ateneo de Manila University
FTP Address: ftp.admu.edu.ph
Directory: /pub/games
Description: Various educational and word games. For a detailed descrip-
                tion of each game read the file "00-index.txt".

FTP Site: ARInternet Corporation
FTP Address: ftp.ari.net
Directory: /pub/MacSciTech
Description: From astronomy to virus protection programs, this archive
                contains hundreds of files and programs for Macintosh com-
                puters.

FTP Site: Center for Innovative Computer Applications (CICA) at
                Indiana University
FTP Address: ftp.winsite.com
Directory: /pub

Description: A clearinghouse archive for Microsoft Windows applica-
              tions, software utilities, drivers, etc. Programs are divided
              into categories.

FTP Site: Coast to Coast Software Repository
FTP Address: ftp.coast.net
Directory: /mir04/SimTel
Description: The Coast to Coast Software Repository is a large archive of
              shareware software for various types of computers. Select
              your computer type from the /mir04/SimTel directory.

FTP Site: Department of Education
FTP Address: ftp.ed.gov
Directory: /gopher/software
Description: The Department of Education maintains a very nice archive
              of educational shareware and freeware programs and games.
              Once in the "/gopher/software" directory, select the direc-
              tory that is appropriate to your type of computer.

FTP Site: Gatekeeper
FTP Address: gatekeeper.dec.com
Directory: /pub
Description: Many useful files and programs for educators and students in
              the pub directory.

FTP Site: Oakland Archives
FTP Address: oak.oakland.edu
Directory: /pub/simtelnet
Description: A large shareware archive for Mac, PC, and UNIX users.

FTP Site: Splicer FTP Server
FTP Address: splicer2.cba.hawaii.edu
Directory: /educatio
Description: Math shareware programs for PC users.

FTP Site: Unicamp: Universidade Estadual De Campinas (Site is in
              English)
FTP Address: ftp.unicamp.br
Directories: /pub5/garbo

/pub5/garbo/mac (for Macintosh users)
/pub5/garbo/pc (for PC users)
/pub5/garbo/windows (for Windows users)
/pub5/garbo/unix (for Unix users)

Description: A very large computer software archive. In the /pub5/garbo directory, select the directory that suits your computer system: Macintosh, PC, or Unix. In each of these directories you will find computer software sorted into categories.

FTP Site: Washington University Public Domain Archive
FTP Address: wuarchive.wustl.edu
Directory: /pub
Description: A very large shareware and freeware archive site. Contains files, programs, games from general purpose use to educational. Files and programs are divided into Macintosh, Windows, and Windows95 categories, then separated by subject. The directory "edu" is of greatest interest to educators and students. Also look into the "mirror" directories; they contain archives of shareware and freeware from around the world.

Space

Information, text files, space history, and images.

FTP Site: Ames Space Archive
FTP Address: explorer.arc.nasa.gov
Directory: /SPACE
Description: Information regarding space history, various space voyages and research, as well as planetary information are archived here.

FTP Site: Center of Resources and Information, Rennes University, France
FTP Address: ftp.univ-rennes1.fr
Directory: /pub/Images/ASTRO
Description: Images from and of space-related objects in JPG and GIF formats.

FTP Site: NASA Jet Propulsion Laboratory's Public Information FTP Archive
FTP Address: ftp.jpl.nasa.gov

131

Directories: /pub/images
                 /pub/fsheets
Description: Images and informational text files of various space-related objects.

FTP Site: NASA Spacelink's Anonymous FTP Server
FTP Address: spacelink.msfc.nasa.gov
Directories: /About.Spacelink
                 /Educational.Services
                 /Instructional.Materials
                 /NASA.News
                 /NASA.Projects
Description: NASA Spacelink provides current information to teachers and students. In the About.Spacelink directory, download the file "Spacelink.Directory.Map". This file contains a complete listing of all the directories and files on the FTP site.

Social Studies

Files pertaining to the social studies field, geography, and culture.

FTP Site: Finnish University and Research Network
FTP Address: ftp.funet.fi
Directory: /pub/culture
Description: Information on various culture, languages, and social movements.

FTP Site: Leibniz Research and Super Computing Center of the Bavarian Academy
FTP Address: ftp.lrz-muenchen.de
Directory: /pub/culture
Description: Information files on the cultures of east-Asia and east-Europe.

FTP Site: Project Hermes
FTP Address: ftp.cwru.edu
Directory: /hermes
Description: Here you will find a large archive of supreme court cases. See

the file "index" for information on the cases currently available.

FTP Site: US Census Information
FTP Address: ftp.census.gov
Directories: /pub(1,2,&3)
Description: Surf around all pub directories. There is a wealth of census information available to the public on the US governmental FTP archive.

Gopher Sites of Interest to Teachers and Students

The following list of gopher sites of interest to teachers and students is by no means complete. It is, however, a list of gopher sites that you may find useful in the field of education. In each case the site address is provided along with any menu information that you will need. Each menu is separated by a backwards slash (/). For example, to reach the menu for "Academic Resources by Subject" at the University of Maryland Information Server, you would first go to the Gopher address of "info.umd.edu". From the *"Main Menu"* you would move to the *"Education Resources"* menu. This will present you with a new gopher menu, where you will find the option entitled *"Academic Resources by Subject."* In the menu information provided here this transition from one menu to another is written like this: *Main Menu/Education Resources/Academic Resources by Subject.* Each backwards slash (/) is an indicator for a menu title option.

Gopher Sites to Get You Started

Gopher Site: Boulder Valley School District and the Internet
Address: bvsd.k12.co.us
Menu Option: Main Menu/

Gopher Site: Dalhousie University's Gopher
Address: ac.dal.ca

Menu Option: Main Menu/Library and Research Resources/ Social Sciences Resources/Education/Resources of Educational Interest

Gopher Site: Educational Gophers from the Library of Congress
Address: marvel.loc.gov
Menu Option: Main Menu/The Global Electronic Library (by Subject)/ Social Sciences/Education

Gopher Site: The Eisenhower National Clearinghouse for Mathematics and Science Education
Address: enc.org
Menu Option: Main Menu/

Gopher Site: ERIC Clearinghouse on Information & Technology, The AskERIC Service for Educators
Address: ericir.syr.edu
Menu Option: Main Menu/

Gopher Site: The Global Electronic Library at the Library of Congress
Address: marvel.loc.gov
Menu Option: Main Menu/The Global Electronic Library (by Subject)

Gopher Site: Mississippi State University
Address: gopher.msstate.edu
Menu Option: Main Menu/Resources of Interest to YOUR Field of Study

Gopher Site: North Carolina State University Libraries
Address: dewey.lib.ncsu.edu
Menu Option: Main Menu/NCSU's "Library Without Walls"/Study Carrels (by Subject)

Gopher Site: Northwest Regional Educational Laboratory (NWREL)
Address: gopher.nwrel.org
Menu Option: Main Menu/

Gopher Site: Rice University Information on Gopherspace
Address: riceinfo.rice.edu
Menu Option: Main Menu/Information by Subject Area

Gopher Site: University of Denver
Address: omercury.cair.du.edu
Menu Option: Main Menu/Other Gophers/The Global Policy Mall/Education

Main Menu/Other Gophers/The Global Policy Mall/Learn America

Gopher Site: University of Maryland Information Server
Address: info.umd.edu
Menu Option: Main Menu/Education Resources/Academic Resources by Subject

Gopher Site: University of Minnesota Computer & Information Services
Address: k12.ucs.umass.edu
Menu Option: Main Menu/

Gopher Site: The University of Texas at San Antonio
Address: nysernet.org
Menu Option: Main Menu/Reference Desk

Gopher Site: US Department of Education /OERI
Address: gopher.ed.gov
Menu Option: Main Menu/

Art and Music

A Veronica search on the key phrase "art and music" produced a list of more than 16,000 gopher sites. Key words "art museum" yielded another 156 gopher sites. A few from these lists and others follow.

Gopher Site: Music at Mississippi State
Address: gopher.msstate.edu
Menu Option: Main Menu/The Internet: "Something for Everyone"/Music

Gopher Site: Nation Museum of American Art
Address: nmaa-ryder.si.edu
Menu Option: Main Menu/

Gopher Site: University of Denver
Address: omercury.cair.du.edu
Menu Option: Main Menu/Other Gophers/The Global Policy Mall/The Arts

Gopher Site: The University of North Carolina at Chapel Hill and Sun Microsystems
Address: sunsite.unc.edu
Menu Option: Main Menu/Worlds of SunSITE—by Subject/The American Music Resource

Gopher Site: The University of Texas at San Antonio
Address: nysernet.org
Menu Option: Main Menu/Reference Desk/700—Arts & Recreation

Education and the Internet

The follow gopher sites contain information on the Internet. Some of the recommended menu options deal specifically with education and the Internet. Others contain helpful information on the Internet, its function, protocols, and history.

Gopher Site: Dalhousie University's Gopher
Address: ac.dal.ca
Menu Option: Main Menu/Guides to the Internet

Gopher Site: The Electronic Frontier Foundation
Address: gopher.eff.org
Menu Option: Main Menu/

Gopher Site: Frequently Asked Question About Gopher
Address: lausd.k12.ca.us
Menu Option: Main Menu/HELP: GOPHER FAQ's (Frequently Asked Questions)

Gopher Site: Guides to the Internet
Address: dewey.lib.ncsu.edu
Menu Option: Main Menu/NCSU's "Library Without Walls"/Reference Desk/Guides (to subject literature, to Internet resources, etc.)

Gopher Site: Search the Lists of Lists
Address: sunsite.unc.edu
Menu Option: Main Menu/Internet Dog-Eared Pages (Frequently used resources)/Search—List of Lists

Gopher Site: University of Denver
Address: omercury.cair.du.edu
Menu Option: Main Menu/Other Gophers/The Global Policy Mall/The Internet

Gopher Site: Using Gopherspace from Michigan State University
Address: gopher.msu.edu
Menu Option: Main Menu/Help Using Gopher (More About Gopher)

Geography

Gopher Site: CIA World Fact Book On-Line
Address: hoshi.cic.sfu.ca
Menu Option: Main Menu/David See-Chai Lam Centre for International Communication/
1994 CIA World Fact Book

Gopher Site: North Carolina State Libraries
Address: dewey.lib.ncsu.edu
Menu Option: Main Menu/NCSU's "Library Without Walls"/Study Carrels (organized by subject)/Geography

Gopher Site: The Peabody Museum of Natural History at Yale University
Address: gopher.peabody.yale.edu
Menu Option: Main Menu/

Health

Gopher Site:	University of Denver
Address:	omercury.cair.du.edu
Menu Option:	Main Menu/Other Gophers/The Global Policy Mall/ Health Information

Gopher Site:	The USU Extension Test Gopher Server
Address:	extsparc.agsci.usu.edu
Menu Option:	Main Menu/Selected Documents (Utah State Extension)/Fact Sheets/Food and Nutrition

History

Gopher Site:	Historical Documents at the University of Denver
Address:	dewey.lib.ncsu.edu
Menu Option:	Main Menu/NCSU's "Library Without Walls"/Study Carrels (organized by subject)/History

Gopher Site:	Historical Text Archives at Mississippi State
Address:	gopher.msstate.edu
Menu Option:	Main Menu/Resources of Interest to Your Field of Study/College of Arts and Science/History

Gopher Site:	North Carolina State Libraries
Address:	omercury.cair.du.edu
Menu Option:	Main Menu/Other Gophers/The Global Policy Mall/Historical Documents
	Main Menu/Other Gophers/The Global Policy Mall/US Speeches and Addresses
	Main Menu/Other Gophers/The Global Policy Mall/History

Gopher Site:	The Peabody Museum of Natural History at Yale University
Address:	gopher.peabody.yale.edu
Menu Option:	Main Menu/

Gopher Site: Smithsonian Institution's Natural History Gopher
Address: nmnhgoph.si.edu
Menu Option: Main Menu/

Gopher Site: Social Sciences and History Documents Found on the
                Queens Library Gopher
Address: vax.queens.lib.ny.us
Menu Option: Main Menu/Social Science & History/Historical Docu-
                ments

Gopher Site: The University of California at Berkeley Museum of Pale-
                ontology Gopher and Natural History Exhibits
Address: ucmp1.berkeley.edu
Menu Option: Main Menu/

Lesson Plans and Curriculum Resources

A search done at a Veronica search site with the key words "lesson plans"
yielded a list of 143 gopher sites with lesson plan and curriculum resources
for education. Some of my favorite sites are listed here.

Gopher Site: Boulder Valley School District
Address: bvsd.k12.co.us
Menu Option: Main Menu/Educational Resources/Assorted Lesson Plans

Gopher Site: Catholic University of America
Address: vmsgopher.cua.edu
Menu Option: Main Menu/Special Resources/ERIC Clearinghouse on As-
                sessment and Evaluation/K12 Resource/K-12 Curriculum
                Resources

Gopher Site: ERIC Clearinghouse on Information & Technology
                The AskERIC Service for Educators
Address: ericir.syr.edu
Menu Option: Main Menu/Lesson Plans

Gopher Site: NASA K-12 Interactive Projects—Take Your Classroom to Other Worlds.
Address: omercury.cair.du.edu
Menu Option: Main Menu/Other Gophers/The Global Policy Mall/ LearnAmerica/Lesson Plans
Main Menu/Other Gophers/The Global Policy Mall/ LearnAmerica/Lesson Plans/NASA Curriculum Plans

Gopher Site: University of Minnesota Computer & Information Services
Address: k12.ucs.umass.edu
Menu Option: Main Menu/

Literature

Gopher Site: Electronic Books
Address: gopher.micro.umn.edu
Menu Option: Main Menu/Libraries/Electronic Books

Gopher Site: Electronic Journals and Books
Address: dewey.lib.ncsu.edu
Menu Option: Main Menu/NCSU's "Library Without Walls"/Electronic Journals and Books

Gopher Site: The Poetry of Yeats, Shakespeare and More
Address: sunsite.unc.edu
Menu Option: Main Menu/Internet Dog-Eared Pages (Frequently used resources)/ Poetry for searching (all of Yeats and Shakespeare plus more)

Gopher Site: University of Denver
Address: omercury.cair.du.edu
Menu Option: Main Menu/Other Gophers/The Global Policy Mall/ Children's Literature

Main Menu/Other Gophers/The Global Policy Mall/ Creative Writing

Main Menu/Other Gophers/The Global Policy Mall/Books Online

Gopher Site: University of Maryland Information Server
Address: info.umd.edu
Menu Option: Main Menu/Education Resources/Academic Reading Room

Gopher Site: The University of North Carolina at Chapel Hill and Sun Microsystems
Address: sunsite.unc.edu
Menu Option: Main Menu/Worlds of SunSITE—by Subject/Poetry and Creative Writing Materials for Browsing and Searching

Math

Gopher Site: The Eisenhower National Clearinghouse for Mathematics and Science Education
Address: enc.org
Menu Option: Main Menu/

Gopher Site: North Carolina State University Libraries
Address: dewey.lib.ncsu.edu
Menu Option: Main Menu/NCSU's "Library Without Walls"/Study Carrels (organized by subject)/Mathematics

Parent Information

Gopher Site: Dalhousie University's Gopher
Address: ac.dal.ca
Menu Option: Main Menu/Library and Research Resources/ Social Sciences Resources/Education/Resources of Educational Inter-

est/Family Education/Children Youth Family Education
Research Network (CYFERNet)

Gopher Site: Department of Education
Address: gopher.ed.gov
Menu Option: Main Menu/Search this Gopher by Key Words (Jughead)/
               Search all U.S. Department of Education Menus Using
               JUGHEAD
               Enter Key Word "PARENT"

Gopher Site: University of Denver
Address: omercury.cair.du.edu
Menu Option: Main Menu/Other Gophers/The Global Policy Mall/Chil-
               dren and Families

Gopher Site: The USU Extension Test Gopher Server
Address: extsparc.agsci.usu.edu
Menu Option: Main Menu/Selected Documents (Utah State Extension)/
               Fact Sheets/Family Life
               Main Menu/US Government Services/USDA Children,
               Youth and Family Education Network

Science

Gopher Site: The Eisenhower National Clearinghouse for Mathematics
               and Science Education
Address: enc.org
Menu Option: Main Menu/

Gopher Site: NASA Space Shuttle Information and Images
Address: sspp.gsfc.nasa.gov
Menu Option: Main Menu/

Gopher Site: North Carolina State University Libraries
Address: dewey.lib.ncsu.edu
Menu Option: Main Menu/NCSU's "Library Without Walls"/Study Car-
               rels (organized by subject)

Gopher Site: Northwestern University: Images from Space, Planetary
                and Lunar Objects
Address: gopher.earth.nwu.edu
Menu Option: Main Menu/Planetology Resources

Gopher Site: The Periodic Table of Elements
Address: sunsite.unc.edu
Menu Option: Main Menu/Internet Dog-Eared Pages (Frequently used re-
                sources)/Periodic Table of the Elements

Gopher Site: The Weather Machine Gopher Server
Address: wx.atmos.uiuc.edu
Menu Option: Main Menu/

Shareware and Freeware Archives

Gopher Site: Department of Education Software Archives
Address: gopher.ed.gov
Menu Option: Main Menu/Educational Software

Gopher Site: FTP Software Archives Via Gopher
Address: hoshi.cic.sfu.ca
Menu Option: Main Menu/FTP Software Archives Via Gopher

Gopher Site: North Carolina State University Libraries
Address: dewey.lib.ncsu.edu
Menu Option: Main Menu/NCSU's "Library Without Walls"/Software
                Tools

Social Studies

Gopher Site: Geographic Name Server
Address: sunsite.unc.edu
Menu Option: Main Menu/Internet Dog-Eared Pages (Frequently used re-

sources)/Search Geographic Name Server by City or ZIP Code

Gopher Site: Search the CIA World Fact File
Address: sunsite.unc.edu
Menu Option: Main Menu/Internet Dog-Eared Pages (Frequently used resources)/Search CIA World Fact Book

Gopher Site: UNICEF Gopher Server:
Address: hqfaus01.unicef.org
Menu Option: Main Menu/

Gopher Site: University of Denver
Address: omercury.cair.du.edu
Menu Option: Main Menu/Other Gophers/The Global Policy Mall/White House Information
               Main Menu/Other Gophers/The Global Policy Mall/Global Issues
               Main Menu/Other Gophers/The Global Policy Mall/World Fact Book

Gopher Site: The University of North Carolina at Chapel Hill and Sun Microsystems
Address: sunsite.unc.edu
Menu Option: Main Menu/Worlds of SunSITE—by Subject/US and World Politics

Gopher Site: The USU Extension Test Gopher Server
Address: extsparc.agsci.usu.edu
Menu Option: Main Menu/US Government Services/The White House

Veronica and Jughead Search Sites

Gopher Site: Boulder Valley School District
Address: bvsd.k12.co.us
Menu Option: Main Menu/Internet Searching Tools

Gopher Site: Gopherspace
Address: lausd.k12.ca.us
Menu Option: Main Menu/Searching Gopherspace using Veronica

Gopher Site: Internet for California's Central Valley
Address: gopher.ainet.com
Menu Option: Main Menu/Jughead Menus (via Ontario, Canada)
               Main Menu/Search Gopherspace using Veronica (UMN)

Gopher Site: University of Denver
Address: omercury.cair.du.edu
Menu Option: Main Menu/Other Gophers/The Global Policy Mall/
               Search the Internet

Gopher Site: University of Minnesota Computer & Information Ser-
               vices
Address: k12.ucs.umass.edu
Menu Option: Main Menu/Other Gopher and Information Servers

Gopher Site: US Department of Education / OERI
Address: gopher.ed.gov
Menu Option: Main Menu/Other Education Gophers and VERONICA
               Searches

Gopher Site: Washington and Lee University in Lexington, Virginia
Address: liberty.uc.wlu.edu
Menu Option: Main Menu/Finding Gopher Resources

World Cultures

Gopher Site: University of Denver
Address: omercury.cair.du.edu
Menu Option: Main Menu/Other Gophers/The Global Policy Mall/Cul-
               ture
               Main Menu/Other Gophers/The Global Policy Mall/Na-
               tive Americans
               Main Menu/Other Gophers/The Global Policy Mall/The
               Americas

146

Gopher Site: The University of North Carolina at Chapel Hill and Sun Microsystems
Address: sunsite.unc.edu
Menu Option: Main Menu/Worlds of SunSITE—by Subject/Welsh Language and Culture Archive

World Wide Web Sites of Interest to Teachers and Students

This appendix is by no stretch of the imagination an exhaustive search for sites that may interest educators, parents, or children. It does, however, contain some excellent links that my classroom has found entertaining and useful. Three sections deal with "Homepages and Web Resources." The addresses referenced in these sections are fantastic sites to start your surfing experience. Other categories have been added to speed along your quest for information and resources. I have also included an address to a specific Yahoo page in each category. These addresses will link you directly to the Yahoo search engine page for that category, or you can surf to Yahoo's main page with the address http://www.yahoo.com. If the information you are seeking is not listed in this appendix, search engines are likely to have what you are looking for.

Art

From classical to modern, art can be found on many virtual walls throughout cyberspace. Also see "Museums" for links to museum pages and museum search engines.

ArtsEdge   http://artsedge.kennedy-center.org/artsedge.html

Good Green Fun: Children's Music and Rainforest Ecology   http://www.efn.org/~dharmika

JazzKids   http://www.tiac.net/users/jazzwill

The Louvre Art Museum   http://www.Louvre.fr

M.C. Escher Web   http://www.texas.net/escher

Native American Artists' Home Page   http://www.artnatam.com

The WebMuseum   http://watt.emf.net/wm

Virtual Gallery   http://www.atom.co.jp/GALLERY

World Wide Web Arts Resources   http://www.concourse.com/wwar/
default.html

Yahoo!   Arts   http://www.yahoo.com/Arts

Educational Organizations and Governmental Agencies

Catholic Education Network   http://www.catholic.org/cen

Curriculum Development Projects from the NSF at Yahoo   http://www.
yahoo.com/Government/Agencies/Independent/National_Science_
Foundation__NSF_/Curriculum_Development_Projects

Impact II Web Site   http://www.teachnet.org

Library of Congress   http://www.loc.gov

National Association of Elementary School Principals   http://www.
naesp.org

National Association of Secondary School Principals   http://www.
nassp.org

National Council of Teachers of English (NCTE)   http://www.ncte.org

National Council of Teachers of Mathematics (NCTM)   http://www.
nctm.org

National Council for Geographic Education   http://www.oneonta.
edu/~baumanpr/ncge/rstf.htm

National Council for the Social Studies   http://www.ncss.org

National Education Association (NEA)   http://www.nea.org

National PTA   http://www.pta.org/

National Science Foundation (NSF)   http://www.nsf.gov

Northeast Regional Educational Laboratories   http://www.neirl.org

Northwest Regional Educational Laboratories   http://www.nwrel.org

Odyssey of the Mind   http://www.odyssey.org/odyssey

Public Broadcasting Service NewsHour Online   http://www.pbs.org

Southwest Educational Development Laboratory   http://diogenes.sedl.org

US Department of Education   http://www.ed.gov

Yahoo! Education: Organizations   http://www.yahoo.com/Education/
Organizations

Yahoo! Education: Government   http://www.yahoo.com/Education/
Government

Health and Special Needs

Teaching anatomy, general hygiene? Need information on ADHD? Health education and special needs resources can be found in quantity. The following links may help you find your way.

Children and Adults with Attention Deficit Disorder   http://www.
chadd.org

Marching Through the Visible Man   http://www.crd.ge.com/esl/cgsp/
projects/vm

The NAMES Project (Aids Quilt)   http://www.aidsquilt.org

Parent Violence and Abuse   http://www.mcs.net/~kathyw/home.html

Yahoo! Education: Special Education   http://www.yahoo.com/Education/
Special_Education

Yahoo! Health   http://www.yahoo.com/Health

Homepages and Web Resources Aimed at Parents

These web sites are not only helpful to parents but to teachers as well. A great resources for all adults working with children.

Ask ERIC Virtual Library   http://ericir.syr.edu

Child Safety on the Information Highway   http://www.4j.lane.edu/
InternetResources/Safety/Safety.html

Department of Education Resource Guides for Parents   http://www.
ed.gov/guides.html#parent

Family Planet Headlines   http://starwave.yahoo.com/starwave/family

Kids Com for Parents: Check Out the Site First   http://www.
kidscom.com/parentsplace.html

National Parent Information Network (NPIN)   http://ericps.ed.uiuc.
edu/npin/npinhome.html

National PTA   http://www.pta.org/

ParentsPlace.com   http://www.parentsplace.com

Yahoo! Society and Culture:Children:Child Safety http://www.yahoo.
com/Society_and_Culture/Children/Child_Safety

Yahoo! Society and Culture: Families: Parenting   http://www.yahoo.
com/Society_and_Culture/Families/Parenting

Homepages and Web Resources Aimed at Students

The following web pages were created with kids in mind. They will help
lead a child through an entertaining, educational, and safe Internet journey.

1994 Goodwill Games   http://www.com/goodwill/index.html

BrainTainment Center   http://world.brain.com

Bsy's List of Internet Accessible Machines   http://www.cs.cmu.
edu/afs/cs.cmu.edu/user/bsy/www/iam.html

Carrie's Crazy Quilt: Homepage Collection   http://www.mtjeff.com/
~bodenst/page2.html

The Children's Page   http://www.pd.astro.it/local-cgi-bin/kids.cgi/
forms

City Kids Directory   http://www.slip.net/~scmetro/citykids.htm

Cyberhaunts for Kids   http://www.freenet.hamilton.on.ca/~aa937/Pro-
file.html

CyberKids Launchpad   http://www.woodwind.com/mtlake/CyberKids/
Launchpad.html

Cyberteens Homepage   http://www.mtlake.com/cyberteens

Daniel's Page of Fun   http://www.worldkids.net/kids/daniel

Danny's Kid Page   http://www.indirect.com/www/mcintosh/danny/danny.
htm

The Electric Postcard   http://postcards.www.media.mit.edu/Postcards

Gage Martin's Borderline Cartoon Site   http://www.cts.com/~borderln

Global Schoolhouse   http://www.gsn.org

Internet for Kids   http://www.internet-for-kids.com

Kid's Web Digital Library for Schoolchildren   http://www.npac.
syr.edu/textbook/kidsweb

KID List: CyberSpace Hang-Outs for K12+   http://www.clark.net/pub/journalism/kid.html

KidPub   http://www.en-garde.com/kidpub

Kids Com: A Safe Place for Kids on the Net to Meet   http://www.kidscom.com

Kids Web   http://www.npac.syr.edu/textbook/kidsweb

Kids' Space—Every Kid's Homepage!   http://www.interport.net/~sachi

Kids Sports Network   http://www.texas.net/user/kidsport

Mapmaker   http://loki.ur.utk.edu/ut2kids/maps/maps.html

MeTaVerse   http://metaverse.com

MidLink Magazine for Kids   http://longwood.cs.ucf.edu/~MidLink

Oasis Here and There Kids' Corner   http://www.ot.com:80/kids

Otis Index   Sites for Kids   http://www.interlog.com/~gordo/kids.html

PBS Online   http://www.pbs.org

Personality Profile   http://sunsite.unc.edu/jembin/mb.pl

Plugged In   http://www.pluggedin.org

The Sports Server   http://www.nando.net/SportServer

Sports Virtual Library   http://www.atm.ch.cam.ac.uk/sports/sports.html

Thalia's Funpage   http://www.sci.kun.nl/thalia/funpage/fun_en.html

Uncle Bob's Kids' Page   http://gagme.wwa.com/~boba/kids.html

Vocal Point Online Student Newspaper   http://bvsd.k12.co.us/cent/Newspaper/Newspaper.html

Warner Brothers OnLine   http://www.warnerbros.com

The Weekly Top Ten   http://www.albany.globalone.net/theMESH/liz.html

WiseGuy Interactive   http://com.primenet.com/kids

World Wide Web of Sports   http://tns-www.lcs.mit.edu/cgi-bin/sports

Yahooligans!   http://www.yahooligans.com

Youth Consumers Database   http://www.screen.com/streetcents.html

Homepages and Web Resources Aimed at Teachers

A great place to start any surfing voyage, these web sites list hundreds of web pages geared especially to the education profession. From lesson plans to curriculum, educational reform to professional contacts, the following web sites will get you started and keep you coming back for more.

537 Ed Sites   http://www.esu3.k12.ne.us/districts/millard/centmidd/ central.html

Academy One Educational Resource   http://www.nptn.org/cyber.serv/ AOneP

Anthology, Virginia   http://pen.k12.va.us

The Armadillo's WWW Homepage   http://chico.rice.edu/armadillo

Ask ERIC Virtual Library   http://ericir.syr.edu

Briarwood Educational Network   http://www.briarwood.com

The Busy Teachers WebSite   http://www.ceismc.gatech.edu/BusyT

Carrie's Sites for Educators (Hot Site)   http://www.mtjeff.com/ ~bodenst/page5.html

Cisco Education Archive   http://sunsite.unc.edu/cisco

Child Safety on the Information Highway   http://www.4j.lane.edu/ InternetResources/Safety/Safety.html

Classroom Connect's Education Links of K–12 Educators   http://www. wentworth.com

Computer-Based Education   http://www.uct.ac.za/projects/cbe

Education Media Library HomePage   http://rs6000.nshpl.library.ns.ca/ ~nmacdona/medlib

Educational Technology   http://tecfa.unige.ch/info-edu-comp.html

EdWeb   http://k12.cnidr.org:90

Effective Education   http://www.io.org/~klima/ed.html

Eric's Educational Resource Page   http://www.teleport.com/~links

EuroNet Main Index   http://www.euro.net/index.html

The Future of Teaching Homepage   http://www.nbn.com:80/~branson

General Education Resources at Teleport   http://www.teleport.com/ ~vincer/general.html

Global Schoolhouse Home Page   http://www.gsn.org

InfoList for Teachers   http://www.electriciti.com/~rlakin

Information on Education Grants   http://galaxy.einet.net/GJ/grants. html

K–12 Cyberspace Outpost   http://k12.cnidr.org/janice_k12/k12menu. html

The K–12 Administrator's Connection   http://www.elk-grove.k12.il.us/walwes/A/TAConnection.html

Kid's Web Digital Library for Schoolchildren   http://www.npac.syr.edu/textbook/kidsweb

The Living Schoolbook   http://www.ilt.columbia.edu/k12/livetext/menu.html

Microsoft Focus on K–12   http://207.68.137.43:80/k-12

The Mind's Eye Monster Exchange   http://www.gbn.net/mindseye/monster_gallery/home.html

NASA k–12 Internet Initiative   http://quest.arc.nasa.gov

Netwatchers Cyberzine (Legal Issues on the Internet)   http://www.ionet.net/~mdyer/netwatch.shtml

New Education Web Site   http://pages.prodigy.com/hstat

Other Education Resources   http://info.er.usgs.gov/network/education.html

Plugged In   http://www.pluggedin.org

Princeton Regional School's WWW Homepage   http://www.prs.k12.nj.us

Scholastic Internet Center   http://www.scholastic.com

Small Planet   http://www.smplanet.com

Texas Center for Educational Technology   http://www.tcet.unt.edu

Web Resources for K-6   http://www.csun.edu/~vceed009

Web66   http://web66.coled.umn.edu

WebEd Curriculum Links   http://badger.state.wi.us/agencies/dpi/www/WebEd.html

WEBreview   http://www.ilt.tc.columbia.edu

World Wide Web Servers for Education Hosted at CNIDR   http://k12.cnidr.org/welcome.html

World Wide Web Virtual Library   http://www.w3.org/pub/DataSources/bySubject/Overview.html

WWW for Instructional Use   University Level   http://www.utexas.edu/world/instruction/index.html

WWW Servers for Education   http://k12.cnidr.org

Yahoo!   Education:K12   http://www.yahoo.com/Education/K_12

Interactive Games

It is important to note that Internet games that require direct interaction between two computers on a near continual basis can be extremely slow with modem-type connections. The following games work best with computers directly connected to an Internet server.

Chess Server   http://www.willamette.edu/~tjones/chessmain.html

The Great Peg Game   http://www.bu.edu/htbin/pegs

Hangman   http://www.cm.cf.ac.uk/htbin/RobH/hangman?go

Mr. Spud Head   http://www.westnet.com/~crywalt/pothead

Tugboat's Online Activity Center   http://www.cochran.com/tt.html

Yahoo!   Recreation:Games:Internet Games:Interactive Web Games
   http://www.yahoo.com/Recreation/Games/Internet_Games/Interactive
   _Web_Games

Internet Help Files and Guides

Need a little help getting started, understanding HTML codes, or putting your web page together complete with graphics? Then turn to the Internet for help.

5 Minute Guide to the Internet   http://www.iquest.net/~mjdecap/beginner.
   htm

Argus Clearinghouse   http://www.lib.umich.edu/chhome.html

Educational Resources on the Internet Guide   http://www.dcs.
   aber.ac.uk/~jjw0/index_ht.html

History of Computing   http://calypso.cs.uregina.ca/Lecture

Internet Help Desk   http://w3.one.net/~alward

Internet Resources Meta-Index   http://www.ncsa.uiuc.edu/SDG/
   Software/Mosaic/MetaIndex.html

Internet Tour   http://www.globalvillage.com/gcweb/tour.html

Irresponsible Internet Statistics Generator   http://www.anamorph.com/
   docs/stats/stats.html

MacHTTP Home   http://www.biap.com

Matrix Information and Directory Services   http://www.mids.org

Netiquette   http://www.primenet.com/~vez/neti.html

The Roadmap: Free Internet Traning   http://ua1vm.ua.edu/~crispen/
roadmap.html

UNIX Help for Users   http://unixhelp.ed.ac.uk

WWW Mac Resources   http://www.comvista.com/net/www/WWW
Directory.html

Yahoo! Computers and Internet:Internet:Information and Documentation
http://www.yahoo.com/Computers_and_Internet/Internet/
Information_and_Documentation

Literature and Literacy

From complete literary works to publishing on the Internet to children's literature and literacy information, the following links will show you the way.

Ananse Stories   http://www.nation.org/~krishnar

Banyan Tree Friends (Publishing Kids)   http://sashimi.wwa.com/
~uschwarz/btf/index.html

Books, Books, Books for Children   http://www.phantom.com/
~fairrosa/cb.list.html

Books for Children and More   http//www.users.interport.net/~hdu

Building Blocks to Reading   http://www.neosoft.com/~jrpotter/karen.html

Carol Hurst's Children's Literature Site   http://www.crocker.com/~rebotis/

Children's Literature Web Guide   http://www.ucalgary.ca/~dkbrown/
index.html

Dr. Seuss Page   http://www2.interconnect.net/drseuss/home.html

IBM Writing Project   www.ucet.ufl.edu/writing

Internet Book Information Center   http://sunsite.unc.edu/ibic/IBIC-
homepage.html

KidLit Childrens' Literature Website   http://mgfx.com/Kidlit

KidPub WWW Publishing   http://en-grade.com/kidpub/intro.html

Kids Talk Books   http://www.smplanet.com/bookclub/bookclub.html

The Kids.com   http://www.thekids.com/kids

Library of Reviews   http://www.teleport.com/~kevcro/library/library.shtml

Mark Twain Resources on the World Wide Web   http://web.syr.edu/ ~fjzwick/twainwww.html

Notes from the Windowsill—Children's Book Reviews   http://www. armory.com

The Online Medieval and Classical Library   http://sunsite.berkeley. edu/OMACL

The Polar Express Share   http://www.hmco.com/polarexpress

Purdue Online Writing Lab OWL   http://owl.trc.purdue.edu

Samford University Writing Project   http://199.20.17.120/index.htm

Scholastic Internet Center   http://www.scholastic.com

Yahoo! Arts:Humanities:Literature   http://www.yahoo.com/Arts/Humani- ties/Literature

Math

Also explore sites listed in "Homepages and Web Resources Aimed at Teachers."

AIMS Puzzle of the Month Page   http://204.161.33.100/Puzzle/ PuzzleList.html

Math Appetizers   http://www.cam.org/~aselby/lesson.html

Michigan Gateways   http://www.msu.edu/comptech/gateways

Net Puzzler   http://virtual-ny.com/net.puzzler

Yahoo! Education:Math and Science Education   http://www.yahoo. com/Education/Math_and_Science_Education

Museums Online

Break down the walls of the classroom and take your class on a virtual field trip to museums throughout the world.

Australian National Botanic Garden   http://155.187.10.12/anbg/index. html

Canadian Museum of Civilization   http://www.cmcc.muse.digital.ca/cmc/ cmceng/welcmeng.html

The Computer Museum Network   http://www.net.org/gateway/index.html

The Earth Galleries   http://www.nhm.ac.uk

Exploratorium Museum, San Francisco, California   http://www.exploratorium.edu

Field Museum of Natural History Online   http://www.bvis.uic.edu/museum

Hand's On Children's Science Museum   http://www.wln.com/~deltapac/hocm.html

The Israel National Museum of Science   http://www.elron.net/n_sci_museum

The Louvre Art Museum   http://www.Louvre.fr

Missouri Botanical Garden   http://straylight.tamu.edu/MoBot/welcome.html

Montshire Museum   http://www.valley.net/~mms

Museum of History of Science   http://galileo.imss.firenze.it

Museum of Natural History, Santa Barbara   http://www.rain.org/~inverts

Museum of Natural Science   http://www.hmns.mus.tx.us/hmns/home.html

Museum of Science, Boston   http://www.mos.org

Museums OnLine   http//www.comlab.ox.ac.uk/archive/other/museums.html

National Zoo, Washington, DC   http://www.si.edu/organiza/museums/zoo/homepage/nzphome.htm

Natural History Museum of Los Angelos County   http://www.lam.mus.ca.us/lacmnh

New York's Metropolitan Museum of Art   http://www.metmuseum.org

Ocean Planet from the Smithsonian   http://seawifs.gsfc.nasa.gov/ocean_planet.html

Oregon Museum of Science and Industry   http://www.omsi.edu

Royal British Columbia Museum   http://rbcm1.rbcm.gov.bc.ca

Royal Tyrrell Museum of Palaeontology   http://www.freenet.calgary.ab.ca/science/tyrrell

Science Museum of London   http://www.nmsi.ac.uk

Science Museum of Minnesota   http://www.sci.mus.mn.us

Sea World Online   http://www.bev.net/education/SeaWorld/homepage.html

The Smithsonian   http://www.si.edu

Smithsonian National Air & Space Museum   http://ceps.nasm.edu:2020/ NASMpage.html

Smithsonian National Museum of Natural History   http://nmnhwww. si.edu/nmnhweb.html

Stephen Birch Aquarium Museum   http://aqua.ucsd.edu

The Tech Museum of Innovation   http://whyanext.com/thetech.html

Tennessee Aquarium   http://www.tennis.org

The Texas Memorial Museum   http://www.utexas.edu/depts/tmm

The Virtual Museums Library   http://www.comlab.ox.ac.uk/archive/ other/museums.html

Yahoo! Museums http://www.yahoo.com/Society_and_Culture/ Museums_and_Exhibits

Project-Oriented Web Sites

The following sites can help you get those Internet projects off the ground with helpful hints, ideas, and information.

Adopt a Student Online   http://www.netline.net/~kathy/mbhs.html

Buckman School Web Page   http://buckman.pps.k12.or.us

Computer-Based Education   http://www.uct.ac.za/projects/cbe

Educational Projects   http://pixel.cs.vt.edu/melissa/projects.html

Global Schoolhouse Project Registry   http://www.gsn.org/gsn/proj/ index.html

Global Show-n-Tell   http://www.manymedia.com/show-n-tell

HPCC K–12 Home Page   http://www.lerc.nasa.gov/Other_Groups/ K-12/K-12_homepage.html

Intercultural E-Mail Classroom Connections   http://www.stolaf.edu/ network/iecc

Kid's Web Digital Library for Schoolchildren   http://www.npac.syr.edu/ textbook/kidsweb

KidNews: Get Your By-line Here   http://www.vsa.cape.com/~powens/ Kidnews.html

KidPub   http://www.en-garde.com/kidpub

Kids Did This: Collection of Kids Work   http://sln.fi.edu/tfi/
   hotlists/kids.html

NASA K–12 Program   http://www.lerc.nasa.gov/Other_Groups/K-12/K-
   12_homepage.html

Peace In Pictures: A View of Peace Through the Child's Eye
   http://www.macom.co.il/peace

Purdue Online Writing Lab OWL   http://owl.trc.purdue.edu

World Wide Kids   http://www.transport.com/~wwkids

Yahoo! Education:K-12:Programs   http://www.yahoo.com/Education/K_12/
   Programs

Youth Consumers Database   http://www.screen.com/streetcents.html

Reference Materials

Is your classroom encyclopedia missing a book or two? Not enough the-
sauruses for the whole class? Turn to one of the on-line reference materials
for help.

BBC Networking Club   http://www.bbcnc.org.uk

Britannica OnLine   http://www.eb.com

China News Digest   http://www.cnd.org

The Electric Examiner   http://www.examiner.com

Kid's Web Resources   http://www.npac.syr.edu/textbook/kidsweb/
   reference.html

Libraries & Librarians Ready Reference   http://www.ipl.org/ref/RR/LIB

Library of Congress   http://www.loc.gov

Living Schoolbook   http://www.ilt.columbia.edu/k12/livetext/menu.html

Newslink   http://www.newslink.org

The New York Times   http://www.nytimes.com

The News Page   http://www1.trib.com/NEWS

Quotation Service   http://pubweb.ucdavis.edu/Documents/Quatations/
   homepage.html

The Reference Center   http://www.primenet.com/~hawaii

Research-it!   http://www.itools.com/research-it/research-it.html

Rice University Library   http://chico.rice.edu

The San Francisco Chronicle   http://www.sfgate.com/chronicle/index.shtml

USA Today   http://www.usatoday.com

The Washington Post   http://www.washingtonpost.com

Yahoo! Reference   http://www.yahoo.com/Reference

Science

From natural sciences to computer technology, from animals to volcanoes, the Internet is full of informational science web sites aimed at teachers, children, and anyone with a need to know.

Academy of Natural Science   http://www.acnatsci.org

Academy of Sciences   http://www.chias.org/

Alaska Volcano Observatory   http://www.avo.alaska.edu

Amphibians and Reptiles   http://xmission.com/~gastown/herpmed/salm.htm

Audubon Zoo in New Orleans   http://www-swiss.ai.mit.edu/philg/summer94/new-orleans-zoo.html

Bradford Robotic Telescope Online   http://www.eia.brad.ac.uk/rti

Cascades Volcano Observatory   http://vulcan.wr.usgs.gov/home.html

Computers and Learning Partners, Science Resources   http://www.clp.berkeley.edu/CLP.html

Discovery Centre   http://www.cfn.cs.dal.ca/Science/DiscCentre/DC_Home.html

Earth and Sky   http://www.earthsky.com

The Electronic Volcano   http://www.dartmouth.edu/pages/rox/volcanoes/elecvolc.html

Environmental Education on the Internet   http://nceet.snre.umich.edu/indes.html

Good Green Fun: Children's Music and Rainforest Ecology   http://www.efn.org/~dharmika

Green World of Frogs   http://www.cs.yale.edu/HTML/YALE/CS/HyPlans/loosemore-sandra/froggy.html

Guide to NASA Online Resources   http://nic.nasa.gov/nic/guide

Honolulu Dinosaur Exhibit   http://www.hcc.hawaii.edu/dinos/
    dinos.1.html

The Interactive Frog Dissection   http://curry.edschool.Virginia.EDU:80/
    ~insttech/frog

Journey North: Wildlife Migration   http://www.ties.k12.mn.us/~jnorth

Kinder Garden   http://aggie-horticulture.tamu.edu/kinder/index.html

Leon M. Lederman Science Education Center   http://www.fnal.gov/
    ed_lsc.html

Maggie's Guide to the Internet for Education   http://www.mindspring.com
    /~mconti/maggie.html

Mercury Project   http://cwis.usc.edu:80/dept/raiders

Michigan Gateways   http://www.msu.edu/comptech/gateways

Museum of Paleontology   http://ucmp1.berkeley.edu/exhibittext

NASA k–12 Internet Initiative   http://quest.arc.nasa.gov

NASA Scientific and Technical Information Server   http://www.
    sti.nasa.gov

Nat'l Marine Educators Home Page   http://www.vims.edu/~jahodg
    nmea2.html

National Science Foundation   http://www.nsf.gov

Nebraska Wildlife Sounds   http://ngp.ngpc.state.ne.us/sounds/sounds.html

Newton's Apple   PBS Series   http://ericir.syr.edu/Projects/Newton

Ontario Science Center   http://www.osc.on.ca

Oregon Climate Service   http://ocs.ats.orst.edu

Our World   http://www.nbn.com/~branson/world.html

Paleontology Without Walls   http://www.ucmp.berkeley.edu/exhibit/
    exhibits.html

Raptors Fly Free (Birds of Prey)   http://www.raptor.cvm.umn.edu

Sea Launch   http://www.boeing.com/sealaunch.html

Science Bytes   http://loki.ur.utk.edu/ut2Kids/science.html

Science Museum of Minnesota   http://www.sci.mus.mn.us

Skull Anatomy 4.0   http://www.umdnj.edu/~chamberl/sklanat/sklanat.
    html

Vermont Whales   http://www.uvm.edu/whale/Introduction.html

Viewing Wildlife Across the USA   http://ics.soe.umich.edu/IAPMain

Volcanos   http://vulcan.wr.usgs.gov/photo_list.html

VolcanoWorld Home Page   http://volcano.und.nodak.edu

Weather   http://www.mit.edu:8001/usa.html

Weather from Nat'l Weather Service   http://thunder.met.fsu.edu:80/nws/public_html

Weather II   http://rs560.cl.msu.edu/weather/index.html

Web-Elements   http://www.cchem.berkeley.edu/Table/index.html

Welcome to Weather World   http://www.atmos.uiuc.edu/wxworld/html/top.html

Whales—a K–5 Integrated Curriculum Unit   http://curry.edschool.virginia.edu/~kpj5e/Table.Contents.html

Whale and Dolphin Conservation Society   http://www.glen.co.uk/wdcs

The Whole Frog Project   http://george.lbl.gov/ITG.hm.pg.docs/Whole.Frog/Whole.Frog.html

The Why Files: Science Behind the News   http://whyfiles.news.wisc.edu/index.html

Yahoo! Science   http://www.yahoo.com/Science

Search Utilities

Search Utilities give Internet users the power to find information with some ease. These links will lead you to some of the best search engines on the Internet. Many are search utilities for strictly educational purposes, others are general Web search engines similar to Yahoo!

4th Grade Teachers OnLine   http://www.edenpr.k12.mn.us/forest/Gr4Conn.html

Best of the Newest   http://www.tricky.com/liz

Best of Web'94   http://wings.buffalo.edu/contest

Cisco Education Archive   http://sunsite.unc.edu/cisco

Education Mailing Lists   http://www.citybeach.wa.edu.au/mailarch.html

Galaxy WWW Index to Resources   http://galaxy.einet.net/galaxy.html

Internet Mailing List Navigator   http://catalog.com/vivian/interest-group-search.html

Internet Resources Meta-Index   http://www.ncsa.uiuc.edu/SDG/
    Software/Mosaic/MetaIndex.html

K-12.ed Newsgroups   http://osiris.wu-wien.ac.at/news/k12.ed.html

List of Lists Champion   http://users.aol.com/lolchamp/home.htm

Lycos   http://lycos.cs.cmu.edu

Magellan   http://www.mckinley.com

Net Search   http://home.mcom.com/home/internet-search.html

Newsgroup Search Index   http://www.cen.uiuc.edu/cgi-bin/find-news

Schools on the Net: Addresses to Many Elementary to High Schools
    http://www.sendit.nodak.edu/k12

Schools Outside the USA on the Net   ttp://www.teleport.com/
    ~kevcro/foreign.htm

Web66: World Wide Web School Registary   http://web66.coled.
    umn.edu/schools.html

WebCrawler   http://webcrawler.com

World Wide Web Virtual Library   http://www.w3.org/pub/DataSources/
    bySubject/Overview.html

World Wide Web Worm   http://wwww.cs.colorado.edu/wwww

WWW Servers for Education   http://k12.cnidr.org

Yahoo! Main Index   http://www.yahoo.com

Social Studies, History, and Geography

Take a trip with Columbus, read about a journey around the world, or create a map of the world.

1492: The Ongoing Voyage   http://sunsite.unc.edu/expo/1492.exhibit/
    Intro.html

Around-the-World Journal   http://home.city.net/travel/atwj

CapWeb: A Guide to the US Congress   http://policy.net/capweb

D-Day   http://192.253.114.31/D-Day/Table_of_contents.html

Flags Galore   http://155.187.10.12/flags/flags.html

Friends and Partners: USA and Russia   http://solar.rtd.utk.edu/
    friends/home.html

The Gallery of the Open Frontier   http://www.unl.edu/UP/gof/home.htm

History Happens   http://www.ushistory.com

The Human Right   http://www.umn.edu/humanrts

Interactive Exposes and Politics   http://www.mojones.com

Live from Antarctica   http://quest.arc.nasa.gov/livefrom/livefrom.html

Map Archive   http://192.253.114.31/D-Day/Maps_room/Map_room_
   contents.html

Mapmaker   http://loki.ur.utk.edu/ut2kids/maps/maps.html

Mapquest   http://www.mapquest.com

Martin Luther King   http://www.seatimes.com/mlk/index.html

Mayaquest Live   http://www.mecc.com/mayaquest.html

Mercury Project   http://cwis.usc.edu:80/dept/raiders

Social Sciences Education   http://galaxy.einet.net/galaxy/Social-Sciences/
   Education.html

Time Travel into History   http://www.xmission.com/~gastown/ebb/
   timetrav.htm

University of Michigan Government Documents Center- http://www.
   lib.umich.edu/libhome/Documents.center/docnews.html

US Supreme Court Information   http://www.law.cornell.edu/supct

Virtual Tourist Information   http://wings.buffalo.edu/world

Welcome to the White House   http://www.whitehouse.gov

Women in History   http://www.netsrq.com/~dbois

Yahoo! Social Sciences   http://www.yahoo.com/Social_Science

Yvonne Andres Trip to Africa   http://www.gsn.org/africa

Software

Many software archives that can be found on FTP are coming to the web for greater ease and flexibility.

MECC Software   http://www.mecc.com

Oak Software Repository   http://www.acs.oakland.edu/oak.html

Sausage Software   http://www.sausage.com

Shareware Stockpile   http://www.azstarnet.com/~outlet/swstpile.html

Shareware.com   http://www.shareware.com

SimTel Software Repository   http://www.coast.net/SimTel

Windows World   http://coyote.csusm.edu:80/cwis/winworld/winworld.
    html

Yahoo!   Computers and Internet:Software   http://www.yahoo.com/
    Computers_and_Internet/Software

Space

NASA leads the way through the solar system. Take a trip to Mars, view the Earth from inside a satellite, or view pictures from the Hubble Space Telescope.

Ames Mars Atlas   http://fi-www.arc.nasa.gov:80/fia/projects/bayes-
    group/Atlas/Mars

Challenger Crew Memorial   http://bloomfield.k12.mo.us/christa.htm

Earth Science and Solar System Exploration Division
    http://exploration.jsc.nasa.gov

Earth Viewer   http://www.fourmilab.ch/earthview/vplanet.html

Guide to NASA Online Resources   http://nic.nasa.gov/nic/guide

Hubble Telescope Pictures   http://www.stsci.edu/EPA/PR/95/44.html

Icarus   http://astrosun.tn.cornell.edu/Icarus/Icarus.html

The Latest Hubble Pics   http://www.stsci.edu/EPA/Latest.html

Liftoff to Space Exploration   http://astro-2.msfc.nasa.gov

The Magellan Image Browser   http://delcano.mit.edu/http/midr-help.html

Mars Pathfinder Project   http://mpfwww.jpl.nasa.gov

NASA Homepage   http://www.nasa.gov

NASA K–12 Program   http://www.lerc.nasa.gov/Other_Groups/K-12/
    K-12_homepage.html

NASA Kennedy Space Center Homepage   http://www.ksc.nasa.gov/
    ksc.html

NASA Space Calendar   http://newproducts.jpl.nasa.gov/calendar

NASA Space Shuttle Small Payloads Info   http://sspp.gsfc.nasa.gov

The Planetary Society   http://wea.mankato.mn.us:80/tps

Quest: Nasa's K–12 Internet Initiative   http://quest.arc.nasa.gov/

Space Telescope Science Institute   http://www.stsci.edu

StarChild: A Learning Center for Young Astronomers   http://guinan.gsfc.nasa.gov/K12/StarChild.html

Students for Education and Development of Space   http://seds.lpl.arizona.edu

US Satellite Images   http://www.nova.edu/Inter-Links/misc/satelite.html

Viking Orbiter Image Site   http://barsoom.msss.com

Welcome to the Planets   http://pds.jpl.nasa.gov/planets

Yahoo!   Science:Space   http://www.yahoo.com/Science/Space

Web Design Help Files, Software, and Utilities

Need help with a web page design? Or perhaps a piece of clipart to brighten things up a bit? These links may have what you are looking for.

ClipArt Collection   http://leviathan.tamu.edu/1s/clipart

HyberText Resources   http://www.eastgate.com/~eastgate/Hypertext.html

ILC Glossary of Internet Terms   http://www.matisse.net/files/glossary.html

Jay's Guide to FRAMES   http://www.columbia.edu/~jll32/html/frame.html

RGB Codes at Doug Jacobson's Homepage   http://www.phoenix.net/~jacobson/rgb.html

Running a WWW Service   http://scholar2.lib.vt.edu/handbook/handbook.html

Sams Publishing Page   http://www.mcp.com:80/sams

Sausage Software   http://www.sausage.com

Sound Tools   http://radioworks.cbc.ca/radio/tools/tools.html

WebCom Comprehensive Guide to Publishing on the Web   http://www.webcom.com/html

Web Machine   http://www.vrl.com/Imaging

WWW Mac Resources   http://www.comvista.com/net/www/WWWDirectory.html

Yahoo!   Computers and Internet:Internet:World Wide Web:Page Design   http://www.yahoo.com/Computers_and_Internet/Internet/World_Wide_Web/Page_Design_and_Layout

Yahoo! Computers and Internet:Software:Data Formats:HTML

http://www.yahoo.com/Computers_and_Internet/Software/Data_
Formats/HTML

World Cultures

The Internet has truly brought the world together through an electronic impulse. Learn more about cultures and people throughout your country, continent, and globe.

Africa News Online   http://www.nando.net/ans

Center for World Indigenous Studies   http://www.halcyon.
com/FWDP/cwisinfo.html

Hebrew OnLine   http://www.info.co.il

Indigenous Resources   http://www.tiac.net/users/actaeon/resource.html

Islamic Resources   http://sparc.latif.com/welcome.html

Mexican Magazines   http://www.eng.usf.edu/~palomare/magazines.html

Multicultural Homepage   http://www.yahoo.com/Society_and_Culture/
Cultures

Native American Internet Resources Index   http://hanksville.phast.
umass.edu/misc/Naresources.html

Native Americans and the Environment   http://minerva.cis.yale.edu/
~lisamc/native_env.html

Native Internet Resources   http://kuhttp.cc.ukans.edu/~marc

NativeWeb   http://web.maxwell.syr.edu/nativeweb

Trail Guide to International Sites and Language Resources
http://www.fln.vcu.edu

Tribal Voice   http://www.tribal.com

US Cultural Protection Legislation   http://www.lib.uconn.edu/
ArchNet/Topical/CRM/crmusdoc.html

Web of Culture   http://www.worldculture.com

Yahoo! Society and Culture   http://www.yahoo.com/Society_and_
Culture/Cultures

Common HTML Tags

The following are some of the most basic and most frequently used HTML tags. In each case, the tag is presented with a description of its usage. Attributes can be added to many tags. These optional attributes effect or change the tag use. Many of the more common attributes have been included below.

Tag: <A HREF="URL"> and </A>

Usage: The anchor tag is used to link one web page to another. This tag will create a clickable link on the web browser. When viewers click on the link, they will move to the new URL. The URL is the address of the web page that it has been linked to (ie: http:// . . .). Any text or images between the opening and closing tag will appear on the web browser as a link, displayed in a different color from normal text.

Example: <A HREF="http://www.teleport.com/~kevcro">Click here to visit Room 13</A>

Tag: <B> and </B>

Usage: All text placed between these tags will appear in bold face.

Tag: <BLINK> and </BLINK>

Usage: Text between the two blink tags will appear on the web browser blinking on and off.

Tag: `<BODY>` and `</BODY>`

Usage: Indicates the body of your HTML document.

Attributes: BGCOLOR="RGB" (will change the color of the background using RGB color codes)

TEXT="RGB" (will change the color of the text using RGB color codes)

VLINK="RGB" (will change the color of the visited links using RGB color codes)

LINK="RGB" (will change the color of the nonvisited links using RGB color codes)

BACKGROUND="IMAGE" (will tile a graphic image, where "image" is the name of the graphic file, in the background of the web page)

Example: `<BODY  BACKGROUND="BACK.GIF"  TEXT="000000" VLINK="00FF00" LINK="00FF66">`

Tag: `<BR>`

Usage: This tag will force a line break in the flow of the web document. Similar to the workings of a return key on a word processor or typewriter.

Tag: `<CENTER>` and `</CENTER>`

Usage: All text between these two center tags will be centered on the web browser.

Tag: `<H1>` and `</H1>`

               `<H2>` and `</H2>`

               `<H3>` and `</H3>`

               `<H4>` and `</H4>`

               `<H5>` and `</H5>`

               `<H6>` and `</H6>`

Usage: The above tags control the font size of the text appearing between these opening and closing tags. `<H1>` is the largest font size available for HTML documents, while `<H6>` is the smallest.

Tag: `<HR>`

Usage: This tag will place a horizontal rule, or a line, across your web page.

Attributes: SIZE="#" (controls the thickness of the horizontal rule, the larger the number, the wider the rule)

Tag: <HTML> and </HTML>
Usage: The opening <HTML> tag is placed at the top of all HTML documents, indicating that the document is hypertext. The closing </HTML> is placed at the bottom of the document, indicating the end of the hypertext code.

Tag: <I> and </I>
Usage: All text placed between these tags will appear in italics.

Tag: <IMG SRC="URL">
Usage: This tag will tell the web browser to load a graphic image file into the web document. The "URL" is replaced with the URL location and file name for the graphic image file to be loaded.
Attributes: HSPACE="#" (controls the space horizontally between the image and the next object)
VSPACE="#" (controls the space vertically between the image and the next object)
BORDER="#" (controls the size of the border surrounding the image)
ALIGN="TOP" (controls the alignment of the image on the web document)
ALIGN="MIDDLE"
ALIGN="BOTTOM"
Example: <IMG   SRC="http://www.teleport.com/~kevcro/line10.gif" HSPACE="5" ALIGN="TOP">

Tag: <LI>
Usage: The list tag will create a list by placing a bullet in front of any text line.

Tag: <OL> and </OL>
Usage: An indented ordered list will be created with this tag. Used in combination with the <LI> tag, the ordered list will be numbered sequentially.

Tag: <P>
Usage: This tag will force a page break in the web document. It is similar to the line break but will produce a double spacing effect.

Tag: <PRE> and </PRE>
Usage: Used to keep preformatted text true to its format and line breaks. All text between these two tags will be printed to the web browser as it is seen in the HTML document, complete with spacing and line/page breaks intact.

Tag: <TABLE> and </TABLE>
            <TR> and </TR>
            <TD> and </TD>
Usage: The above tags are used in combination to create a table on the web browser. <TABLE> tag opens the table function. <TR> opens a new row in the table and </TR> closes the row. <TD> is used to control the columns of the table. Textual and graphical information can be inserted between the <TD> and <TR> tags to get the desired table effect.
Example: <TABLE>
            <TR><TD>Row 1 Col 1</TD>
            <TD>Row 1 Col 2</TD></TR>
            <TR><TD>Row 2 Col 1</TD>
            <TD>Row 2 Col 2</TD></TR>
            </TABLE>

Tag: <TITLE> and </TITLE>
Usage: This tag will set the title of your web document. Any text between the opening and closing tags will be printed in the title bar of the web browser.

Tag: <UL> and </UL>
Usage: An indented, unordered list will be created with this tag. Used in combination with the <LI> tag, each line in the list will be preceded with a dot bullet.

Bibliography

Amoto, S., J. Callahan, N. Kerr, K. Pitter, and E. Tilton. 1995. *Every Student's Guide to the Internet*. San Francisco: McGraw-Hill.

Aronson, L. 1994. *HTML: Manual of Style*. Emeryville, CA: Ziff-Davis Press.

Baroudi, C. and J.R. Levine. 1994. *Internet for Dummies*. Foster City, CA: IDG Books Worldwide, Inc.

Caillian, R. 1995. "A Little History of the World Wide Web." Internet WWW site, at URL: <http://www.w3.org/pub/WWW/History.html> (version current 31 Jul 1996).

Cross, W. 1996. *All-In-One Search Page*. Internet WWW site, at URL: <http://www.albany.net/allinone> (version current 31 Jul 1996).

Educational Resources and Information Center. 1996. AskERIC. Internet WWW site, at URL: <http://ericir.syr.edu> (version current 31 Jul 1996).

Gromov, G.R. 1996. "The Roads and Crossroads of Internet's History." Internet WWW site, at URL: <http://www.internetvalley.com/intval.html> (version current 31 Jul 1996).

Hahn, H. and R. Stout. 1996. *The Internet Yellow Pages*. New York: Osborn McGraw-Hill.

Hughes, K. 1994. "Guide to Cyberspace 6.1: How Was the Web Created?" Internet WWW site, at URL: <http://www.eit.com/web/www.guide/guide.04.html> (version current 31 Jul 1996).

Kubaitis, E. 1995. "Find Newsgroups." Internet WWW site, at URL:

<http://www.cen.uiuc.edu/cgi-bin/find-news> (version current 31 Jul 1996).

Matrix Information and Directory Services, Inc. 1996. *MIDS! Homepage.* Internet WWW site, at URL: <http://www.mids.org>. Internet Gopher site, at URL: <gopher://gopher.mids.org> (version current 31 Jul 1996).

Miller, E. B. 1994. *The Internet Resource Directory for K-12 Teachers and Librarians, 94/95 Edition.* Englewood, CO: Libraries Unlimited, Inc.

Orenstrin, R. 1996. *Internet Statistics Generator.* Internet WWW site, at URL: <http://www.anamorph.com/docs/stats/stats.html> (version current 31 Jul 1996).

Pfaffenberger, B. 1994. *Mosaic: User's Guide.* New York: MIS Press.

Ramsthaler, K. 1995. *The List of Lists Champion.* Internet WWW site, at URL: <http://users.aol.com/lolchamp/home.htm> (version current 31 Jul 1996).

Stark, T. 1996. "The Marc Andreessen Interview Page." Internet WWW site, at URL: <http://www.dnai.com/~thomst/marca.html> (version current 31 Jul 1996).

U.S. Department of Education. 1995. "A List of Education-related Mailing Lists." Internet Gopher site, at URL: <gopher://gopher.cic.net:3005/11/listservs> (version current 31 Jul 1996).

U.S. Department of Education. 1995. "USENET Newsgroups." Internet WWW site, at URL <http://www.ed.gov/pubs/OR/ConsumerGuides/usenet.html> (version current 31 Jul 1996).

Vincent, P. 1995. *Free Stuff from the Internet.* Scottsdale, AZ: Coriolis Group, Inc.

Williams, B. 1995. *The Internet for Teachers.* Foster City, CA: IDG Books Worldwide, Inc.

Yahoo. 1995. *Yahoo.* Internet WWW site, at URL: <http://www.yahoo.com> (version current 31 Jul 1996).